CW00970943

AXIS OF THE WORLD

The Search for the Oldest American Civilization

Igor Witkowski

Other Books of Interest:

AXIS OF THE WORLD

Igor Witkowski

Adventures Unlimited Press

Axis of the World
The Search for the Oldest American Civilization

ISBN 10: 1-931882-81-9
ISBN 13: 978-1-931882-81-1

Published by:
Adventures Unlimited Press
One Adventure Place
Kempton, Illinois 60946 USA
auphq@frontiernet.net

www.adventuresunlimitedpress.com

10 9 8 7 6 5 4 3 2 1

AXIS OF
THE WORLD

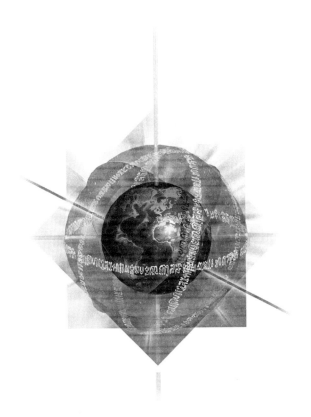

Igor Witkowski is a Polish author and researcher living in Warsaw. He is the author of nearly a dozen books on the history of World War II, and is extremely wellknown in his home country. Witkowksi now turns his attention to the mysterious archeology of the Pacific in *Axis of the World*, his first book in English.

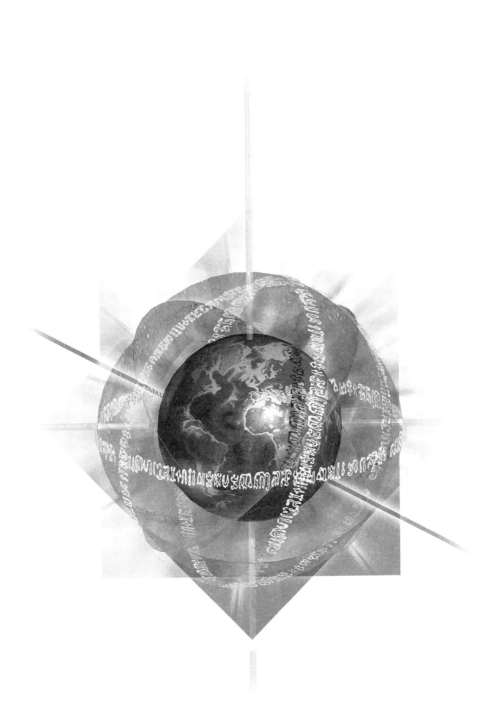

TABLE OF CONTENTS

AXIS
OF THE
WORLD

...the progress of science does not match the discoveries
achieved by previous generations and many of them,
not finished, had been squandered.
— Seneca, *Quaestiones Naturales*, (first century AD)

1

THE REAL MYSTERY
OF EASTER ISLAND

This book pertains to a quite unusual, strange mystery, rooted very deep in our past. It is multidisciplinary, and encompasses facts referring to various continents. It compares archaeological discoveries, ethnological relations, and even the achievements of genetic research. But the stake is, I believe, well worth such a puzzle, for in the end a certain comprehensive picture—albeit one completely different from the standard "academic truth"—emerges. *The picture is that of one of the strangest, almost unknown, yet probably the most interesting civilizations ever existing on our planet.* It is different, although based on very solid, even unequivocal, evidence, and quite hard to "debunk." It has simply been ignored for decades. It has to be emphasized: it is not the conclusions that are ignored, but the facts themselves.

This quest reveals remnants of a high civilization that was able to exert its influence almost on the scale of the entire planet, and did so with full consciousness. America (South America, to be exact) turned out to be not just one of these places, but a crowning achievement in a way. There are several "keys" to this strange riddle, lying in various parts of the world. In some instances they are inconspicuous, but perhaps that's what makes them all the more interesting. Easter Island, in the southeastern Pacific, constitutes one of them.

I went there in March of 1999, although the word "went" doesn't reflect all the drama of the undertaking. From the European perspective (I live in Poland), it's almost the other end of the world. The flight from Madrid to Santiago de Chile alone was the longest non-stop flight that I ever experienced—aboard Iberia's A340-300 (still one of the most state-of-the-art, long range planes ever made, by the way). It lasted over 13 hours! That wasn't all, however. The final leg of the journey was the flight from the Chilean capital to the island—five more hours, almost reflecting the distance, let's say, from Scotland to the eastern provinces of Canada. Why I'm writing about this?

Mainly because Easter Island is associated with the end of the world, the end of everything. It is the most remote and isolated place that one can imagine. It has become almost mythical in this sense.

This reflection is worth remembering for one simple reason. I would even dare to say that it is so simple, that it evades attention of the scientists: A very small island, the size of a not-too-large-city district, almost devoid of resources, the very symbol of isolation, that on the other hand "created" a sophisticated system of writing. This is an unquestionable milestone in development that, for instance, did not evolve in all of North America, despite a far longer period of time at the "disposal" of that continent. Isn't something wrong with this picture? That's a straightforward question that doesn't require any research to ask.

Anyway, I started gathering information and eventually arrived there with a strong suspicion that the island is "something more," part of a larger puzzle if you like.

But what is Easter Island like? Is there presently really any feeling of mystery hovering in the air? Well, my first impression after the arrival was pretty unpleasant. Although it was after dusk, the hot, humid and completely still air was almost overpowering. The temperature was in the mid-eighties range (around 30 °C), but it is generally hard to sleep if there is no air conditioning in the hotel—I doubt if any have it. It is however a civilized land, even with access to the Internet via a satellite dish. The island is a sort of Chilean colony, around 2000 miles (3200 km) distant from its mainland and 27 degrees south of the equator. For this reason the flight is considered domestic and the national carrier, LAN-Chile, has a monopoly and dictates the prices. In this case the ticket was more expensive than for the stretch from Europe to Chile itself—$800. In the case of travel from the US the ratio would certainly be even more disadvantageous. One "way out" is to buy a "combo ticket," i.e. together with the ticket from your country to Chile. By the way: the Chilean airline is excellent in every respect, generally better than the North American airlines. Occasionally LAN flies with their A340s also from Santiago to

14

New Zealand and Sydney, as well as Aerolineas Argentinas—the Argentine carrier, from Buenos Aires (over the Antarctic). In the case of LAN, Easter Island is also a stopover on a flight to Tahiti, so there is an option of getting there that way too. Paradoxically, it makes the tiny airport on that piece of rock a truly cosmopolitan place. A lot of people stop there on their way from Asia to South America and I suspect that they outnumber the original inhabitants. So in this respect the industrial civilization has effectively stripped the island of its mysticism—or just reduced it a little bit.

Nevertheless the place definitely is attractive, regardless of whether someone is aware of the prehistoric context or not. Easter Island is a completely different kind of land than what we generally know. It's a conglomerate of volcanic cones and lava fields, which one can see on almost every occasion. The most important are obviously the remains from ancient times—and not just the famous "Moai" statues—there are so many of them that the entire island with an area of 117 sq. km (around 45 square miles) is in fact a gigantic, open air museum in which, additionally, some exhibits are marked and described. Their number is so great that a week seems to be too short a time to stay. The island is an irresolvable, tiny dot on the map of the Pacific Ocean, but it's definitely too large to make a round of it on foot. It resembles an almost perfect isosceles triangle, approximately 10 by 10 by 15 miles (17, 17 and 24 km respectively). One can see over 200 statues, although initially there were over 900 of them (!), and countless stone platforms called *ahu*. Some of them, like Ahu Vinapu are sheer marvels of precise treatment; natural and artificial caves in which the tablets covered with the *rongo-rongo* script have been found: reliefs, petroglyphs, ancient quarries where the monumental statues were carved out, as well—of course—as the breathtaking landscapes. Despite very poor vegetation—dominated by "freshly" green grass, there are also fragmentary forests—the views are picturesque. A look into the majestic, one kilometer-wide Rano Kao crater, filled with a lake, or the view from the surrounding cliff onto the turquoise ocean are the landscapes that one just will never forget. If we climb up on the centrally located Maunga Terevaka mountain (the island's highest peak, 506 m above sea level—1660 feet), we will experience a truly mystical impression that indeed we are in the navel of the world—as the island's original name reflects. In whichever direction we look, there is only the sky and the ocean stretching up to the horizon. As we can see, even the natural conditions favor the preservation of a certain mysterious aura surrounding the Easter Island.

This aura, however, is completely incompatible with the archeological reality—the mystery dormant or hidden somewhere on the island, stretching far beyond the questions connected with the problem of transporting the huge statues, some of which weigh up to 200 tons. Neither is it about the question of how such an amazing civilization could be created by a population limited to a couple of villages or hamlets—because such a population simply could not create it. It's very hard to imagine the entire chain of events contributing to the development of any civilization to be taking place *only* there. The local soil, for example, is almost nonexistent, consisting only of porous lava which could hardly sustain any sophisticated agriculture. Frankly speaking, one could hardly imagine more disadvantageous conditions, never mind the tropical torpor and the omnipresent ants.

Almost all the researchers identify the riddle referring to this place with the way the stony statues were raised and transported. If we take into account their initial number (see above) and mass— most weigh up to 10 tons, with the record-holder, still lying in the quarry, weighing in at approximately 300 tons—then indeed it will turn out that a genuine problem exists. No doubt that is an unusual phenomenon, but it is not one deserving to be considered "the number one riddle." Even when the conventional explanations sometimes seem far-fetched, it is only a matter of the magnitude of force applied (the number of people) and time. It's a problem that cannot be ignored, but it shouldn't overshadow the true top-rank challenges, and there are several of them.

The least trivial and most important question, the common motif, is this: where did the strange Easter Island culture come from? In turn, as far as the details are concerned, the local writing constitutes the crucial challenge in answering this question. However, it's not only about the issue of decoding the hieroglyphs. The more important issue seems to be the fact that *this writing is a mirror reflection of the writing used thousands of years ago in the*

Indus Valley area, in today's eastern Pakistan. This fact has been known for eighty years and in spite of that, its importance somehow hasn't come to the attention of academic archaeology yet. After all, the fact that traces of some closely related and hitherto unknown culture has been found on opposite ends of our planet—moreover traces that almost do not differ from each other—breaks all the stereotypes pertaining to the migrations of peoples, intercultural contacts, and above all the general knowledge of the Ancient Ones. The issue of navigational knowledge is just a modest example of this.

It's just as if some day we would discover in Alaska a mirror reflection of the Egyptian Great Pyramid. All the foundations of Egyptology we could then, with a clear conscience, throw in the trash bin.

The fact mentioned above confirms quite an obvious conclusion that Easter Island's culture did not originate on this piece of rock itself, but was brought here from elsewhere. That's just the tip of the chain reaching far to the west and deep, to the very beginnings of human history. Deep? Or maybe we should look for these traces on the bottom of the ocean?

It's plain to see that this story recalls all the legends of the lost Pacific continent, which say that several millennia ago there flourished some antediluvian, great civilization… Anyway, only the search for some older, "greater" culture may be considered as a sensible starting point for the understanding of Easter Island's riddle, a riddle much broader and more important than it would seem at first glance. So let's pass on to what we know of the history of this "most isolated" piece of land on our planet, surrounded by the vastness of the largest ocean.

Although the first modern European sailors visited this island as early as 1722, a lot of time had to pass before it could be brought closer to our world. The island had been discovered in the aforementioned year by a Dutchman named Jacob Roggeveen. Because it occurred on Easter Monday, he named it after that holiday and this name survived the test of time, which frankly speaking, is rather the exception to the rule. In later years occasionally it attracted various adventurers, who generally left very bad impressions behind.

Among others, as one of few territories not belonging to any country yet, the island seemed to be an ideal source of "free labor"—slaves, in other words. This illegal practice was initiated by the US schooner *Nancy* in 1805. Its crew kidnapped many Easter-Islanders to hunt seals, and numerous women were also abducted. When after more than a week they were released out of their cages, all of them jumped into the sea. It's hard to say if they were heroic, i.e. committed collective suicide because of the humiliation, or if rather they just didn't realize how big the world really is. In 1801 the American whaling ship *Pindos* anchored here, with an equally tragic outcome.

On the 12th of December, 1862, a flotilla of six Peruvian ships arrived with the intention of abducting people for guano mining (a very valuable fertilizer) on the islands off the coast of Peru. This time it ended up with a massacre, mostly of women and children. Around a thousand Polynesians were kidnapped, including the last "scholars"—priests, as well as the last king—Murata, along with his entire family. Peruvians are still not welcome on the island.

These practices were effectively terminated only in 1888, when Easter Island was proclaimed part of Chile, the country's first and only overseas colony. Eventually it gained certain protection and presently is part of the Fifth Region. The first more or less comprehensive "scientific reconnaissance" of the island was also under Chilean auspices. It took place in 1870 with the arrival of the corvette *O'Higgins*, carrying teams of scientists and cartographers. They made the first map and brought to the continent the first tales of the mysterious statues and other artifacts that shocked the scientific world of the time (albeit the French *La Perouse* made some measurements, and sketches were also drawn as early as in 1786, but it was hardly a scientific activity and largely went unnoticed by science). It wasn't imagined that such an unusual culture could develop on such a "forgotten" and remote piece of land, almost in the middle of the vast ocean.[2]

According to the legends of the Polynesian inhabitants, their ancestors arrived and settled there in "ancient times," led by the first king, named Hotu Matua. There is a myth saying that these people moved on from a "Maori land," lying on the "continent of Hiva." Because it slowly submerged into the ocean, the king

18

summoned up his men and told them to build ocean-going boats, in which they soon departed in the search of a new land. These legends were gathered by many researchers, but the best collection of them is probably the work of the Frenchman Francis Maziere, which was published in the 60s.[1] Maziere interprets it as a clear message referring to the lost Pacific continent, which—according to him—reached the Tuamotu archipelago in the east. The legends also say that the small island—Sala y Gomez lying some 100 miles off the coast of the Easter Island—was once connected with it by a land bridge. If it's true, then it would mean that the colonization took place far, far earlier then it is commonly assumed.[1]

Thor Heyerdahl, the famous Norwegian pioneer of the idea involving transoceanic contacts, came across some record of the Easter Islanders' forgotten legends, including a legend describing the long-gone, sunken Pacific continent, the abode of the pre-civilization. This is one of its fragments:

The young man Tea Waka said:
—In the old times our land was large, very large.
Kuukuu asked him a question:
—Why it turned small then?
Tea Waka replied:
—Uwoke has lowered his stick on it. He has lowered his stick on the Ohiro town. Big waves raised and the land became small. It has been named Te-Pito-o-te-Henua. Uwoke's stick was broken on the Puku-Puhipuhi mountain.
Tea Waka and Kuukuu talked about the Ko-te-Tomonga-o-Tea-Waka village (the place where Tea Waka has reached the shore). Then the Hotu Matua king came ashore and settled on the island. Kuukuu said to him:
—Once this land was greater.
The friend, Tea Waka said:
—The land sunk.
Then Tea Waka added:
—This town is now called Ko-te-Tomonga-o-

Tea-Waka.

Hotu Matua asked:

—Why the land sunk?

—Uwoke did this, he has pushed the land— replied Tea Waka. The land was named Te-Pito-o-te-Henua. When Uwoke's stick was long, the land has collapsed into the abyss. Puku-Puhipuhi—that's how the place where Uwoke's stick was broken is now called.

—The Hotu Matua king said to Tea Waka:

—My friend, it was not Uwoke's stick. It was the thunder of the Make Make god. Hotu Matua has settled on the island.[3]

According to "textbook science" Hotu Matua undertook his quest probably in the 12th century AD. The rub, however, is that according to the new research, Easter Island was inhabited earlier. Thor Heyerdahl, the Norwegian researcher and author of many unorthodox theories referring to the Pacific cultures, came accross— during excavations carried out in 1987—certain traces of human occupation dated a couple of centuries earlier. Probably these were remains of some simple buildings or rather huts.[4] Legends at least partially clear up this mystery. According to them, initially there were two different tribes on the island. The first one was the "Ha-nau-aa-epe"—the "long ears" or "long eared" (please note the syllabic record, the syllables corresponded with the signs of writing). They were characterized by tall height, almost white skin and red hair. They supposedly were almost two meters tall (some 6.5 feet). They controlled the island and formed a "ruling caste," and among other things, they didn't work. The ruled tribe were in turn those whose ancestors can be encountered today: the "Ha-nau-mo-moko"—the "short eared."

The statues were probably carved by the "short eared" under the command of the "long eared," portraying actually the latter ones—which is rather evident. It can be seen not just from the length of their ears, but for example also from their facial features which seem to be closer (if we pass over the artistic manner) rather to the "Europoidal" type—taller faces with relatively long noses. Also their "wigs" are telling in this respect, as they are made from a red volcanic rock. The legend also explains why the statues raised along the shores have their faces turned toward the center of the island (or rather "had," for after the uprising of the short-eared which terminated the history of this culture, all statues along the coast of the island were knocked over and were placed in their original positions only quite recently). Such an inward direction was supposed to guarantee protection of the interior, with the magic force — "mana" — against the destructive power of the ocean, so that it wouldn't take the land away as it did with "Hiva."[1]

The first mention of the coexistence of the two races on the island came from Roggeveen, after his visit in 1722:

> Some had their ears falling up to their shoulders and few of them actually had two white, large balls in their ears, as if some big decoration. (…)
>
> Some locals served their gods more often and with greater dedication and zeal, which forces us to presume that they were priests, all the more that they wore distinctive marks, such as big balls hanging from their ears and had totally shaved heads.

Others, such as Maziere, pointed out to the identicalness of these customs with the Marquesas Islands.

All researchers of Easter Island were, however, fascinated with the uncanny statues and especially with the way they were carved and transported. Many diverse theories were put forward, and generally speaking, many of these were as fanciful as those put forward in the case of the building of the Great Pyramid. The quite simple, and most obvious hypothesis, that referring to transporting the statues on wooden rollers or logs, didn't stand the test of time for a variety of reasons, the most obvious being the lack of a sufficient number of trees, as well as insufficient resistance to transverse loads. If you put a match on the floor and try to roll over it with a shoe's sole, it will turn into sawdust pretty quickly. It is a justifiable comparison, since most of the statues, or "moais," weigh, as has been calculated, almost 10 tons. One statue still resting in the quarry may weight up to 300 tons, which is a mass of some three locomotives.

The most valuable probable hypothesis was developed by a certain Czech engineer, who came to a conclusion that it would be easiest to move them in the following way: tilt a statue slightly to the right, turn it clockwise (forward), tilt it to the left and turn anticlockwise, continuously pushing forward. It seems sensible for the simple reasons that, firstly: according to the locals the statues "walked on their own" and secondly: their bottom parts bear the marks of chip-offs that occurred apparently after they were carved out. It is also worth noticing that according to the legend the stony giants moved "on their own," to designated places thanks to the magical power called "mana." Regardless of whether it's true or not, it is, however, nonetheless a fact that the same type of description of motive power emerges in the "second best" place of archaeological mystery in the Pacific, namely Nan Madol — some 10,000 km away to the west (around 6200 miles). Later on we will see that it's not the last such a similarity between these two strange places.

However, this is by no means the end of puzzling parallels. The mana power was symbolized by a sign that perhaps was supposed to concentrate it, and which was carved out on the backs of some statues. Strangely enough, it bears a striking similarity to the Egyptian magic "ankh" cross, which was supposed to perform the same function.

If we have already been captivated by this mythology, then it's worth raising the issue of the peculiar cult which flourished on Easter Island — the cult of the "bird-men." It is by no means clear where it came from. According to numerous researchers and the local legend as well, it supposedly was the consequence of the old, megalithic cult of the bird's egg on the one hand (and in particular, of the special role of a bird which was set free after spotting Easter Island in order to bring this happy news to the sinking continent Hiva). In my view, however, this doesn't explain the factors which contributed to this cult's origin. And if we take into account that it wasn't limited just to Easter Island, but occurred in the Andes as well (in present Bolivia which was documented extensively by Heyerdahl), and that over a quite large area, we have to admit the possibility that it originated earlier than it is assumed in reference to Easter Island itself.[4] It could also have originated somewhere else as well. Anyway, it is the first quite solid piece of evidence, but not the last, which indicates common elements in the Andean and Pacific cultures. We should also bear in mind that something resembling a man-bird hybrid, some peculiar god, occurs also as a hieroglyph in Easter Island's mysterious Rongo-Rongo writing. There's no doubt that it's a very important element which not only proves that there were links with the Andean civilizations (or at least with one of them), but which should also be used to trace the islanders' culture back to its roots. The issue is all the more interesting in that it undermines the prevailing theories on the peopling of the Americas—theories that prevail especially in North America to such an extent that they have become a kind of scientific, quasi-religious dogma. The force of the human mind's inertia is, and will long be, a very powerful one. We will, of course, return to these roots later.

Presently, or to be more precise, until very recently, the islanders cultivated the custom of annual races for the first egg layed on the nearby, tiny islands of Motu Iti and Motu Nui. It is tied with the legend of the Make Make god, who was the lord "of all creatures living in the sky," hence a bird could be one of his symbols. One may always adopt the typical explanation of saying that a god, by definition a being that descended on Earth "from above" was simply symbolized as someone with wings (as in the ancient cultures there was no distinction between flying creatures and flying devices—there were no such ideas in their thesauruses—just as there was no distinction between "sky" and "heaven"). Yes, but the actual truth turns out to be more interesting than that. We will return to this issue, obviously.

The race itself served the purpose of selecting a man, who for a given year became the god's personification and bearer of the divine mana, the magic force associated with Make Make. During this time, as a taboo, he was isolated from his family and sealed off in a cave or a specially prepared hut, in order for the lack of sunshine to make his skin brighter and hence more god-like. But he was supposedly isolated not just for this reason, but also because his enhanced mana could be... dangerous. The legend quoted by Maziere describes the times when Make Make lived among the people, yet. His mana was allegedly so powerful that his clothes *"were so shining that he was like a cloud, framed by a rainbow."* Many researchers attempted to unravel both the term "mana," as well as the origin of the mysterious "cross with a circle," placed on some statue's backs. It was ascertained that the word itself probably originates from the area of today's India, where it is still in use, and with—naturally—the same meaning (!). The same is the case with the cross. An identical symbol found in India is known as "kundalini" (life force), and there is also a Chinese equivalent, where it is described as "the door of life." In all these cases the meaning is similar, if not identical. And identical motifs occur in other cultures as well. Regardless of our understanding of this phenomenon, then, we should in my opinion notice especially the effect of luminosity, mentioned in reference to Make Make. Myths from all over the world all say generally the same thing in this case: when they describe the gods that descended from the sky/heaven, otherwise resembling us. The Bible alone could provide several such descriptions. And saints, for example, were always portrayed with luminous aureoles, and this was the case in the Christian tradition, as well as in the Hindu.[1]

The unequalled Soviet researcher of so-called lost civilizations, Alexander Kondratov, states that Make Make's main attribute was lightning—exactly the same motif associated with the main Andean god, Virakocha.[3] I have to admit that while visiting Tiahuanaco, in Bolivia, I saw reliefs practically identical with the images of Make Make from the Easter Island: round face with large, circular eyes and a thick line of the nose smoothly connected with wide eyebrows. We will return to these analogies again.

Francis Maziere quotes one more intriguing legend in his book, heard while he was on Easter Island. According to one of the present inhabitants:

> The first people who settled on the island were those who survived from the first race on our planet. With a yellow skin, very tall, with long arms, wide chests, giant ears—but not stretched, very bright hair, as well as shining bodies, not hairy.[1]

According to the myths—and science fully confirms this—the present inhabitants, not counting the newcomers that arrived from Chile, are the descendants of the former "short-eared" race. As it is presently assessed on the basis of archaeological datings, around 1760 (i.e. after Roggeveen's visit) a battle between the tribes of the ruled and ruling ones occurred. This was the uprising I referred to previously. Long suppressed animosities finally found an outlet:

> The island was ruled by the Ha-nau-aa-epe, the "long-eared." It was they who built the Ahus [stone platforms]. The people with short ears used to work for them. After all the stones from the Poike peninsula had been thrown to the ocean, the "long-eared" ordered the same to be done on the whole island, so to be able to sow everywhere…
>
> The Ha-nau-mo-moko refused to carry out this order, claiming that they needed the stones to bake the food and for better cultivation of the taros. Facing the refusal, the "long-eared" retreated to Poike, where they dug up a big trench in anticipation of the attack [across the peninsula], which they filled up with branches, the stalks of reeds, and grass.
>
> The attack then followed, and the "long-eared" set the trench on fire and defended themselves, although they had no chances anyway. Some of them probably died directly during the clash, while the rest "were surrounded and knocked off the rock, which at the end of a natural rift protrudes over the Hotu-iti. There they were massacred and baked in a big furnace named Ko-te-umu-o-te-hanau-eepe. Their land had been burned and a great cannibalistic feast took place."

According to this tradition, the rulers lost because there were few of them left at this time—around one hundred. After these events, apparently in an act of posthumous revenge, all the Moai statues were knocked over or destroyed. The ones that stand up presently have been, as I mentioned, placed in their original positions in modern times, by the Chileans. Roggeveen and his men were the last "outsiders" who saw the original social order on the island.

Traditionally the statues were placed on special stone platforms, called Ahu, and Ahu Vinapu is considered the most perfect one. It lies in the southeastern corner, at the foothills of the Rano Kao volcano, just by the eastern end of the airport runway. What was emphasized by many researchers, including scientists, is that it represents exactly the same style of stone-cutting and construction as the monumental Andean ruins, such as Tiahuanaco (Tiwanaku); Ollantaytambo; the Incan ceremonial center (not a fortress!) of Sacsayhuaman; and Machu Picchu. What is worth noting here, of these similarities, is that:

1. The stone blocks are very closely matched to each other, despite rounded, complex shapes;
2. They are polygonal;
3. Their external surfaces are convex; and,
4. The entire wall is inclined toward the center of the construction.

This last feature is especially interesting, for in the Andes (and perhaps in other locations in the Pacific, which we don't know about) it served the purpose of protecting against the effects of earthquakes, as did the curved sides closely matching each other. On Easter Island however, there were no significant earthquakes in recorded history.

Generally, the Ahu Vinapu platform is a very strong argument speaking for the close connections with South America, or rather with specific spots there. So close, that they had to take place in historic times.

Of course, it's just the first example in an entire chain of similarities in technical, linguistic, religious and other realms. The Island has been named by the locals the "navel of the world." Curiously enough the Island of the Sun, lying on Lake Titicaca on the Andean plateau and playing a crucial role in the Incan legends pertaining to the origin of their civilization, also bears the exact same name (as if the Incas, living high in the mountains, were a nation of islanders). They used virtually the same totora reeds for the making of reed boats identical to those that were used by the population of Easter Island for fishing, despite the fact that the reed occurred only in a small lake inside one of the volcanic craters.[4, 5]

In 1956 Thor Heyerdahl and his expedition excavated one of the "crown proofs" of these affinities: a statue different than from moai in that it portrayed a complete figure, one with legs. It depicts a kneeling man, quite unique in appearance. Among other things, it's a figure of a bearded man. There are very few similar statues in the world: one has been found in Mohenjo Daro (a center of the aforementioned Indus valley civilization, where a mirror reflection of the Easter Island writing has been found), and two specimens in the central Andes, in Bolivia, close to the aforementioned Lake Titicaca and Tiahuanaco! These also have beards, although Indians of Siberian or northern origin have no facial hair! One of them stands in the Tiahuanaco museum, and the other in the Bolivian capital, La Paz. So again, as in the case of the writing, we have a clear indication that Easter Island was in fact closely tied with other cultural centers of the ancient world, even extremely remote ones. However, even though the facts are undeniable, "official" archaeology doesn't accept them, not because they have been successfully "debunked," but because they not only would cause the collapse of entire theories and dogmas, but above all because the consequences of these facts are enormous! They form a comprehensive, well grounded, although very strange picture, challenging our entire understanding of the remote past (and the American past in particular). But what about the other pieces of the puzzle?

These analogies point not only to the high Andes. For example: the stone axes, known in Polynesia as "toki," bear the same name in the Chilean Araucania (which lies far to the south of the continent, some 500 km or 300 miles south of the country's capital). There is, moreover, one place in South America where the similarities to Easter Island's culture are "concentrated" and, to put it simply, just striking. It's Tiahuanaco, located high in the most unfriendly, dry and cold part of the Andes. It gives us something that resembles a chain of traces: Mohenjo Daro (in today's Pakistan), Easter Island itself and Tiahuanaco—over 2300 miles or 3700 km farther to the east. However, this presents a certain problem, namely that Mohenjo Daro and its Indus Valley civilization literally vanished from the archaeological scene around 1000—1200 years B.C. It means that at the moment when Easter Island was inhabited, Mohenjo Daro's unique system of writing, its religion, etc. (the bearded statue probably represents some god) lived only in human memory. It has been gone for over two millennia (at least according to officially accepted theories)! It was simply one of the three oldest civilizations on our planet, along with the Sumerians and the empire of the pharaohs. Could Easter Island's culture reach that deep into the prehistory of mankind? Incidentally, these circumstances make the Rongo Rongo script the oldest system of writing in use in historical times, for no less than four thousand years (although nobody can be sure if it was used continuously). In the case of this chain of traces, the truth seems so obscure, and so strange at the same time, that one has to ask himself a question: what really happened there, in the Pacific and the Indian Ocean, all those thousands of years ago? And last but not least: who were these people?

These are by no means trivial questions. As I mentioned, "official" science still pretends that they don't exist…

In the next chapters, information will be presented which points to yet another center of this culture, another link in the chain if you like: Nan Madol, perhaps the strangest ruin in the world.

One of the questions that potentially may help us clear up this picture is of course the one referring to the aforementioned writing. We will return to this also.

As I mentioned, research and other studies explicitly prove that there were two completely different migrations to the Island, of two different peoples. The latter ones are the Polynesians, speaking basically the same language that is in use on other Polynesian islands. In terms of "cultural baggage" they share it generally with other Polynesian peoples. The earlier one, however—that of the "long eared"—was of different origin (called Protopolynesians). They had, among other things, more elongated, taller skulls, brighter skin, and of course, a very different cultural heritage. They spoke a non-Polynesian language and according to the known tradition, it was they and only they, who knew the secret of writing. After the aforementioned massacre of the "long eared," around 1760, only three of them survived. In spite of that, at the moment of the arrival of the Europeans and Chileans there was a vast store of Rongo Rongo tablets and other wooden artifacts covered with these hieroglyphs—hundreds at least. They were carefully kept in special covers made of reed, although the ability to read them was gradually vanishing, and worse, later on the white colonizers, and especially the local missionaries, lit bonfires with them. The oldest reports about the existence of this writing brought the second European expedition, after Roggeveen's voyage. This time it was a Spanish ship, whose mission was to take over the island for the Spanish crown. This was in 1770. Its commander, Captain Gonzales, wanted to comply with all the formalities, and prepared a special act. He was literally left speechless when the local chief signed this document with his name![3] The fact that at the bottom of this paper appeared a signature, albeit hieroglyphic, was not only shocking, but it also shattered all the knowledge current at that time, based on the Eurocentric view of the world—not to mention the fact that the island was so remote. That the great civilizations of the New World developed advanced systems such as writing independent of the old continent was quite an unimaginable then. This notion of the alleged superiority of European culture (ultimately meaning the "white race") was of course inherited from the Middle Ages. It was all the more baseless, since during these Middle Ages Western Europe rejected the great cultural, and to a large extent technological, heritage of the Romans, Greeks and even the Arabs, all of which represented higher levels of development. In medieval western Europe whole areas of research such as the medical sciences or chemistry were virtually nonexistent due to ideological considerations. Rationalism as a way of perception was effectively rejected and to such an extent that the Ptolemaic model of the world and the Solar System (or more accurately, the "Earthly System," for in this case the Earth was its center) was generally accepted for well over a millenium, despite the fact that observations clearly contradicted it. According to this model Venus should occasionally be on the other side of the sky from the Sun, which obviously never happened because it's always closer to the Sun than the Earth. Despite that, observed facts were treated as secondary because of the close relationship between science and Aristotelian ideology, "ideological correctness" if you like. I am writing this because I'm aware that the facts presented in this book, especially those presented in the next chapters, may trigger quite a similar response: rejection not because they are inaccurate, but because they do not match certain preconceived views. Sometimes I have the impression that we live in the "New Middle Ages," by the way. But the story and the issue described here is not about cultured animosities. In my view it's a moral question, for first and foremost, it's a pursuit of the truth.

But let's go back to Easter Island.

The first European who settled on the island permanently was the French priest, Eugene Eyraud, and it was precisely he who initiated the campaign of burning the priceless "Kohau Rongo Rongo" tablets. In his description of the Island he recorded also that the inhabitants encountered by him (in the mid 19th century) were unable to read this writing.[2] This confirms the fact that the "long eared" kept this knowledge for themselves as a closely guarded secret, much like Mayan and Egyptian priests kept to themselves the knowledge of eclipses in order to exercise their power.

According to the legend, the first king, Hotu Matua, brought with him 67 most precious tablets from their land of origin in the west.[7] We can only suppose that they contained the "core" of their religious, and perhaps historical texts. It is also known that he brought the religion tied with the "bird-man" and with Make Make. It has generally nothing in common with the different variants of purely Polynesian beliefs, based on the cult of the Tane and Kon Tiki gods. All in all, presently we know of 26 various genuine artifacts covered with the Rongo Rongo hieroglyphs. They contain around 16,000 signs in all. Thus, contrary to appearances, there is quite a lot of material to study.[7]

These are mostly tablets which earlier were hidden in caves and caverns (mostly underground beds carved out by flowing lava). Despite a widely advertised offer made by the government of Chile, which offers tens of thousands of dollars for any newly discovered artifact containing the Rongo Rongo writing, nothing new has emerged.

This writing has a certain unique feature, characteristic

exclusively to it, the identical Mohenjo Daro scripts as well as certain evolved variations used on a small scale on the Andean altiplano: it is namely a method of writing known as "bustrophedon," from the Greek meaning "like a plowing ox," i.e. alternately from left to right and from right to left. After recording one line the writer turned the tablet upside down, and kept writing, "like a plowing ox."

Easter Islanders and statue as depicted in the "Voyage of La Perouse."

31

The fine stonework at the wall of Vinapu on Easter Island.

The fine stonework at the wall of Vinapu on Easter Island.

Indus Valley	Easter Island	Indus Valley	Easter Island	Indus Valley	Easter Island	Indus Valley	Easter Island
I	II	III	IV	V	VI	VII	VIII

A portrait of one of the long ears of Easter Island.

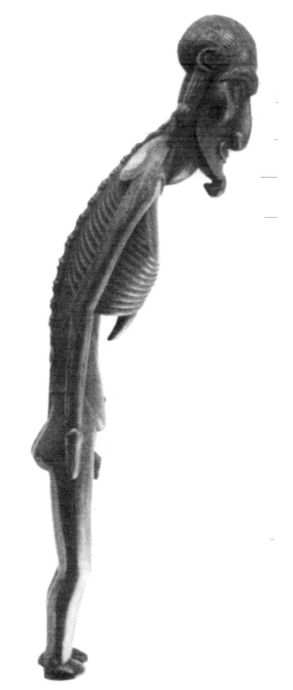

A wooden Kava Kava statue from Easter Island.

Rongo-Rongo wrtiting from Easter Island.

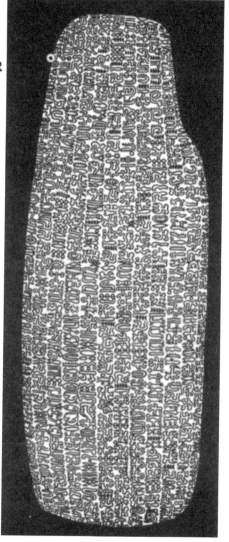

Top: Writing from New Zealand.
Right: Rongo-Rongo wrtiting from
Easter Island.

An Orongo birdman from Easter Island.

An Assyrian birdman from ancient Mesopotamia.

2

PROFESSOR SZALEK'S BREATHTAKING DISCOVERIES

My first meeting with Professor Benon Z. Szalek from the University of Szczecin (in Poland) was the result of a rather strange event and generally accidental. He read one of my previous books, in which I touched upon the topic of Easter Island's mysteries, after which he sent me a letter with a demand to correct a certain piece of information. I had neglected to mention him as the "decoder" of the Rongo Rongo writing. For my part it was a totally unintended mistake; I knew nothing about my fellow countryman's discoveries. I write about this because to this day very few people, even in Poland, know of these discoveries and realize their groundbreaking character. However, as a result of the aforementioned, unpleasant misunderstanding, I was able to establish contact with Professor Szalek, which turned out to be fruitful and interesting. He sent me a selection of his publications on the subject, and I conducted an interview.

The challenge that constituted the starting point of his studies—which eventually ended up in success and made the whole journey all the more intriguing—was the identification of the similarities between Indus Valley writing (Mohenjo Daro being unofficially considered its capital) and the Rongo Rongo script. Unraveling this unusual mystery led him not only to the reading of the hieroglyphs, but furthermore to a series of no less significant findings, findings that explained, at least partially, where the connections encompassing almost our entire planet come from. Facts were brought to light that knocked the issue of the ancient civilization out of the realm of guesswork and placed it in the context of specific knowledge.

But let's start from the beginning…

It was obvious that the attempt to decipher the mysterious writing must be preceded by ascertaining the respective spoken language and the nation or people which used it. Knowing the spoken language was essential for reading the writing. Moreover, the knowledge of the specific people that used it should contribute knowledge of its cultural influences, migrations, etc. In any case, Professor Szalek was confronted with a task (or confronted himself with the task) of analyzing an enormous quantity of linguistic data, and that in many languages.

Attempts to decipher hieroglyphs left by extinct civilizations are, as we know from history, problems on which many researchers have blunted their teeth in the past, regardless of their linguistic knowledge. Yuriy Knorozov, who decoded the Mayan scripts and spent, along with others, a lot of time in such an endeavor. By the way: he was just an army officer who found the Mayan *codices* in the ruins of some shelled German library and devoted part of his life to deciphering something that many western scholars didn't see as a writing at all—just "pictures." He didn't manage to read the Rongo Rongo script.

I dare to say that Professor Szalek turned out to be a truly outstanding person in this respect. Frankly, my professional activities give me an opportunity of meeting many interesting people, but Szalek is the only one whom I may call, with clear conscience, a genius. Although he probably would never admit it, that's just a simple conclusion drawn from the results of his work; even his first approach to the problem is telling. Here's how he recalls this initial phase himself:

> On some sunny afternoon in 1961, I spotted a small volume in a window of one of Szczecin's bookstores… It was entitled *Forgotten Writings and Languages*—written by J. Friedrich. On that evening I immersed myself into the world of mysterious writings left by the long-gone civilizations of Egypt, Sumer, Asia Minor. Thanks to Friedrich's book, for the first time I could see the inscription on the Phaistos disc, writings of the Indus Valley civilization as well as the mysterious signs from Easter Island. I realized then that unraveling of the mysteries of the past requires expertise in many foreign languages—

both dead and alive. In elementary school we were taught Russian and German, but these beginnings were not enough to understand specialist books on archaeology, history and linguistics. I started therefore an intensive self-learning of foreign languages. In 1971, when I was finishing studies in one of Szczecin's universities, I could read belles-lettres as well as specialist literature in 20 languages, including Russian, Ukrainian, German, English, French, Italian, Spanish, Portuguese, Latin, Old-Greek and Japanese.

I started learning Japanese on my own in 1970. A year later I wrote a letter with hieroglyphs for professor Nagano in Tokyo and in 1973 I was granted a job as an interpreter in a Japanese Ataka company, exhibiting its products at the International Fair in Poznan. [7]

Although it may seem strange at first, it was precisely this ability to read and understand many languages that unveiled before Professor Szalek the threads leading to the "super-civilization" from many thousands of years ago. Only after revealing the linguistic connections and relationships did the possibility of decoding the writing emerge. The truth loomed into view very slowly; it was a toilsome job, and initially nothing indicated that a chain of events fraught with consequences had begun.

It started with the necessity of translating certain specialist publications written in the Hungarian language. It was 1974, and the Professor already possessed a rich comparative basis—he knew a lot of languages, including Japanese. Pretty quickly an amazing fact was unveiled—namely it turned out that Hungarian had many common features with Japanese! It was quite a discovery. Although it was known for a long time that both languages were counted among the so-called Finno-Ugric group of languages, nonetheless at that time, the prevailing view was that Japanese was not related to any other language, not to mention any European one!

Here I owe my American readers a certain explanation. The languages of Europe are divided into two distinct groups, or to be more precise, two completely different groups that (omitting certain exceptions) have almost no common elements. The first group constitutes all the languages that you have probably heard about. But the other group includes languages such as Hungarian, Finnish and Basque (Basques live in the northern provinces of Spain and are considered *the oldest* ethnic group in Europe). The differences between these two language groups are truly fundamental and they clearly point to the possibility that there were two migrations to Europe, of two very different peoples of different origin. As we can see, the latter group has, at least linguistically, more in common with the Japanese than with its European neighbors. According to my encyclopedia, the Finno-Ugric nations represent *"the pre-Indoeuropean migration, preceding the influx of other peoples."* What Professor Szalek initially noticed was therefore important in the respect that it tells us about some "other" branch of the white population, *older and with slightly different roots.*

The similarities discovered by him in 1974 did not refer to specific words, but to the grammatical structure of entire phrases in general—however strange it may seem. For example: the phrase "he was beating a good cow" in Hungarian is written as "jö üszöt üttöt," while in phonetic transcription from the Japanese, is it "joi usi o utta." "To light a fire" is "hev surol" in Hungarian and "hi suru" in Japanese. It also turned out that the Finnish and Basque languages fit into the scheme.[7,9]

The following is an example—a comparison of some Hungarian and Japanese words, plus their English meaning:

Hungarian	Japanese	English
kor	koro	the time
jo	joi	good
josag	josa	goodness
görög	koroga-	to roll
mind	mina	all
okoz	okosu	to initiate
hatar	hotori, atari	the vicinity
hatar	hata	the edge
haborog	abareru	to go mad, to revel
zavar	savaru	to disturb

ür................uro.......................the emptiness, empty
homok...........hama....................the sand, sandy shore

It's similar to Basque:

Basque	Japanese	English
hatse	hatsu	the beginning
eme	me	female
ume	umi	the birth
ager toki	agaru tokoro	the place of appearance
anaia	ani	the brother
ana	ane	the older sister
bai	hai	yes
kitto	kitto	exactly so
tori!	toro!	take!
da	da	is
hori bakarrik	kore bakari	exactly this one

It already seems sensational that such unrelated nations—as it may seem—that evolved under completely different condition and that represent different races (!) and that live on different continents, turn out to have such common cultural roots. What sort of process could lead to such a situation?

Professor Szalek came to the conclusion (and it appears that it's the only possible explanation) that these peoples must have been subjected to the influence of some single state organism—or that they were once part of it. It would have to be a civilization more powerful than any of the historic states known to us if its influences are noticeable in spite of such a scale of distance, time and all the other factors. Of course, we don't know of any such a civilization from human culture's formative period which could have exerted such a global influence, even if only indirectly.

Why I have written about the initial period of our history, or even prehistory? For the simple reason that on the basis of the anthropological, archaeological and linguistic knowledge we can relatively precisely ascertain the time "window" after which there was certainly no cultural exchange anymore between the Japanese and their colleagues from Europe. It could not be more recent than approximately 7000 years ago![7]

But it's not quite the end of the story yet. In the course of research spanning almost ten years, Professor Szalek proved that this mysterious "family of nations" consisted also of the Dravidians and Tamils—peoples that once lived in the Indus Valley! In this case the similarities are equally striking:

Japanese	Tamil	English
iru	iru	to be
kuru	kuruku	to come
naru	naralu	to sound
pune, fune	pune	the boat, ship
ha-pa-ba	ha-pa-ba	the tooth
kiru	kiri	to cut
naru	neru	to happen
niru	ner	to be similar
katana	katakam	the sword
katari	katai	the tale
wakeru	wakir	to divide
otiru	utir	to fall

The Dravidians had also separated from the aforementioned group of nations around 7000 years ago. It is an astounding fact that they are representatives of the black race! And of course science does not recognize any prededent of one culture imposing itself upon the members of four such different peoples. That's at least how Professor Szalek perceives it. But in my view, this didn't have to be necessarily the case, for that civilization itself could probably exert strong influence upon various ethnic groups that were more or less "tied" with its cultural circle, but wouldn't have to constitute inherent parts of it. Some could be tied more, some less, some for a longer period (i.e., would have joined it earlier) or for a shorter period. In either case, there's no doubt that it's a complex issue, probably without a single straightforward answer.

According to the Professor's views, the Indus Valley civilization would not be the source of this culture, but rather it was the one that had successfully preserved and developed the older heritage. This is how he himself has described it:

46

It follows from my "glotto-chronological" research* that the empire formed by the linguistic community, "three peoples—one language," (we may designate it as the "3=1 empire" for short) *existed until approximately 7000 years B.C.*** The analyses led us to conclude that *this writing was known at the times of this empire*. It is indicated by the fact that in the languages of the Tamils, Japanese, as well as in the Finno-Ugric languages the core -ir, -sir, -ir means "to write or to draw." Official science claims that first systems of writing appeared on the scene some *3000 years later*— around 4000 B.C.

Perhaps the echo of this empire rings in some Asian legends. In the Hindu, Tibetan and Mongolian tradition, for example, appears the memory of some "golden age" state, about the "kingdom of happiness" and the rule of holy sages and yogis. Some—for example Sri Aurobindo—claim that the then masters could crush rocks with the voice and were able "to locate the Sun in darkness."

There are known reports on the findings, in Asia, of ancient human skeletons characterized by a level of radioactivity 50 times higher than average.*** Perhaps the lords of the 3=1 empire created an alternative civilization and were able to utilize other, non-mechanical ways of influencing their environment. Perhaps the legendary Agharta (= Shambala) is identical with the 3=1 empire...

The outcome of my studies is such that around 7000 B.C. the 3=1 empire broke up. The glotto-chronological research indicates that the Finno-Ugric peoples were the first that disconnected from the group. [7]

It seems therefore that the Mohenjo Daro writing (which equals the Easter Island writing, remember) was used by the Dravidians

47

who lived in the valley of the Indus river and it represents the oldest system of writing on our planet, although probably evolved to some extent. It could not have evolved and diversified too late however, because its variants, which are found in such remote parts of the world, are virtually identical. It proves then that at the moment when the various ethnic "offshoots" disconnected from each other and chose various directions of migrations (literally spreading the "word"), it was already developed and did not differ significantly from the writing that we know today—and that's a huge challenge to our understanding of history itself!

It re-invokes the question of how it was possible that a writing (along with the religious elements of tradition) has emerged on Easter Island when the Mohenjo Daro culture was forgotten for at least a couple of thousand years. The honest answer is simply that nobody has even the slightest idea how it was possible, especially taking into account the fact that it's exactly the same writing. But regardless of the speculations, we must come to the conclusion that there must have been *some* continuity, *somewhere*. We don't know where yet; perhaps the mystery of Nan Madol holds some relevant niche, in which the culture could have been preserved for some time. (Nan Madol will be described later.) But we also have to be open to the possibility that the migrations in the Pacific area have a slightly older history than we think they have.

The totality of facts presented above is significant because *only in its light we can see that Easter Island's mystery and the mystery of its writing is something truly special*—a kind of "key" to our past, and to the past of America—as we will see later. The presence of this writing in such different parts of our world *cannot be explained by some accidental contacts*—let's say from 15th century A.D.—as official science would like to see it! Incredible, isn't it? How is it possible that our civilization functions at all? This simply cannot be the case, because it's a writing of a long extinct civilization predating the 15th century by thousands of years, the oldest one on our planet! Unraveling this riddle will therefore not be merely an ethnographical or linguistic curiosity, but it will constitute a key to the origins of human culture in general. It is a precious key at that, inasmuch as probably no-one has illusions as to the extent of our present knowledge about this part of our history. Basically there is no comprehensive knowledge of this part of it. If, however, someone has still some doubts, please consider the following discussion of Professor Szalek's other amazing discovery.[10, 11]

The fact that the writings from Easter Island and the Indus Valley are practically the same constitutes, as I mentioned, an insurmountable challenge for archaeology and anthropology in general due to the huge distance separating these places. But that's not all yet, *for both places are located symmetrically in relation to the equator and practically in opposite points on the globe* (Mohenjo Daro as the center of the Indus Valley civilization and Easter Island). The geographic latitude is basically the same (respectively 27° 11' S and 27° 17' N)—the difference is an error of merely 0.02%! Slightly larger is the error in the case of longitude—two and a half degrees, or 1.4%. In the terrain it corresponds to the distance of around 250 km (155 miles), which is a very small value when compared to the overall distance—or half of Earth's circumference on the equator— slightly over 20,000 km or 12,420 miles. A truly global achievement! What ambition! Or rather—what far-sighted planning, for there can be no doubt that none of their contemporaries could have ever even noticed that! And the same question is raised again: who *were* these people?

In light of the facts we may therefore rule out coincidence, especially if we take into account that it's the only such a case on our planet. The straight line connecting these two points we may name an "axis of the world." By the way, it is also questionable to consider the inaccuracy as an error. After all, the city of Mohenjo Daro was certainly established earlier than the "messengers" of the super-civilization reached Easter Island—it was just the closest piece of land to the place where "the axis" passed through the surface of our globe. Exactly—globe! The authors of this undertaking must have realized that Earth is a sphere, have precisely known its dimensions, the location of its equator, and so on! At these times even that was an example of "culturally incompatible" knowledge—something that had no right to exist *at that time*, or to be produced by the culture as we know it. It is "an impossible fact." Or to put it more frankly, it is "an impossible technology!" After all, so-called conventional knowledge totally rules out the possibility that people then (even people of only a thousand years ago, as science would like to see it, would be able to determine such precise geographic coordinates in order to correlate two points lying on opposite sides of the Earth!

It seems impossible, but it finds confirmation in the form of other discoveries. In one of Kondratov's books (an outstanding Soviet scholar) I found the following fragment:

> In 1968 the Buryatsian Branch of the Soviet Academy of Sciences's Siberian Department published the third edition of the Materials for the History and Philology of Central Asia. One of its articles in this volume was devoted to Buddhist cosmology. Apart from the traditional views (not differing much from the one that the Earth rests "on three elephants") there existed in Buddhism—especially in the tantric one—a completely different notion on the structure of the Universe; and in the tantric "kalachakra" system, where Earth has the shape of sphere rotating around its axis. It's hard not to agree with the article's author, R. Pubayev that "all is undoubtedly interesting from the scientific point of view"… Incidentally, according to the Buddhist ideas humans are descended from apes and their humanization has taken place in today's India. [3]

Professor Szalek pointed out, in turn, two facts confirming the non-coincidental character of the "axis of the world." Firstly, it arouses reflection that the writing of both cultures, on opposite side of the world, are mirror reflections of each other. It seems as if the "architects" of the axis wanted to convey something to us. Secondly, apart from Easter Island there is one more, previously mentioned, mysterious center of an unknown civilization. It's Nan Madol, in the Federated States of Micronesia—some 1200 miles or 1900 km to the northeast from Papua New Guinea and over 1700 miles to the northeast from the Australian coast. Nan Madol has strange ruins, nicknamed "the Venice of the Pacific," for they are divided by countless canals.

Of course, it's not just the fact that they exist, but that they are located *exactly in the middle of the line connecting Mohenjo Daro and the island of the stone giants!* This time the placing is almost ideal as far as longitude is concerned, but as to the latitude, an error of couple of hundred kilometers appears. Here too, we may adopt the hypothesis that the "error" was the result of the lack of an island in the mathematically determined location. "Nan Madol" sounds quite mysterious, but for professor Szalek it has a specific meaning. He has noticed that this strange name gains sense when we assume that it is pronounced in one of the Dravidian languages. It then means nothing less than *"in the middle of the way"*!

And that's an irrefutable proof that thousands of years ago a civilization existed that consciously realized measures on the scale of the entire globe. If we connect that with the deciphering of the writing, then it would be quite hard to imagine a more momentous "group of discoveries" concerning human history.

The paradox consists in the fact that until very recently these matters were completely unknown, even in Poland! Professor Szalek mentioned in the meantime that when he delivered a lecture, in 1984, on the deciphering of the mysterious hieroglyphs, only four listeners came, including two colleagues from his institute.

Exactly—it's high time to pass on to the description of the crucial decoding itself.

As I mentioned previously, this writing has certain unique features: the so-called bustrophedon—or writing alternately from left to right and from right to left; it did not display any clear analogies to other decoded writings; there often appeared the hieroglyph symbolizing the "bird-man." Because apparently it was the oldest writing on Earth (or at least as old as the Sumerian and Egyptian writings) it resisted any decoding attempts for a long time.

The way in which my fellow countryman from Szczecin did this is a very complex process. His publication describing the process c omprises two volumes and approximately 800 pages in all, so it's not possible to repeat the whole of this book.[8] I'm presenting therefore only a brief synopsis.

Naturally the logical asumption was that it was a record corresponding to one of the Dravidian languages, as it was precisely they who created Mohenjo Daro and Harappa—the two cities where the oldest tablets were found. The first step on the way to decoding this writing was the grouping of all the known signs. It then turned out that they do not connect with each other coincidentally, but that certain combinations dominate, presumably corresponding with certain most often used words, names or religious formulas. After all that, however, it wasn't so simple, for the reason that over 3000 different hieroglyphs were identified. Apart from that, copies of the inscriptions reproduced in the literature contained errors and all had to be additionally verified. After identifying the most often appearing combinations of signs, Professor Szalek noticed in turn that in certain instances a given sign was replaced by another—while the rest of a certain common combination of signs remained the same. It looked as if certain signs could be used alternately. For example the *bird* hieroglyph was sometimes replaced by the sign portraying a bird with a broken neck, or a man holding his cut-off head in his hand. It happened that the *crescent Moon* sign was replaced by the *arrow* sign, and so on.

It suggested the presence of so-called homonyms—ambiguous signs or terms, or more precisely, syllables that were "shorthands" for words having identical or very similar phonetic sounds.[7,8] There was no shortage of such examples, while the following homonyms occured most often:

1.   *bird = death* or *dead,*
2.   *fish = star,*
3.   *crescent Moon = arrow = cross,*
4.   *head of a shouting man = turtle's head.*

Having at his disposal the earlier indications pointing toward the Dravidian languages, Professor Szalek assigned the "alternate" hieroglyphs to the ambiguous words occuring in one of them—in the Tamil language. As he has written himself:

> In the Tamil language there exist words matching the following set of equations (with capitals corresponding to the actual sounding of the signs or words, not to their appearance):

1. WII = bird = death,
2. MIIN = fish = star,
3. AMBULI = Moon; AMBU = arrow; WAMBU = cross.

This was already a concrete key. First and foremost it was known to what spoken language the writing corresponded. Also obviously significant the fact that the graphic portrayals reflected, at least to some extent, the meaning of the respective words or syllables. Apart from that, it was also proven that it's a syllabic writing. As Szalek wrote:

> These observations became the starting point for the decoding work, which lasted through the years 1984-1987. In February of 1987, on a public lecture, I presented the outcome of these works. I will describe them below in a possibly synthetic way.
>
> The Easter Island inscriptions are made with a writing originating from the Indus Valley civilization. Both are syllabic writings. In both the signs had their names, whose first syllables constituted the phonetic values of the signs...
>
> Apart from the conformity, however, the sets of syllables also display certain differences. For example—in the Easter Island writings the sign from the Indus Valley probably portraying a "horse" does not occur. It has been replaced by the "blade" sign (in the Tamil language both words have a similar sound—WARI or WASI). The KA syllable is represented not by the "hand" sign—as in the Indus Valley—but by the KAA syllable and the "turtle" or the "lame man" sign (the words sound similar in the Tamil, respectively: KALLI and KAAL'LI—hence their interchangeability).
>
> The Easter Island writings surprise one with the variety of their signs, which suggests that my claim about their syllabic character is incorrect. I

53

will try to explain however, as it is only possible, that it is only with the aid of the set of syllables consisting of several dozen simple signs that such "baroque," ornate texts could be created. I even had the impression that the copyists expressed in this way how keen they were to add variety to the scripts, as if they wanted to grace the subject of their cult.

Firstly, then: they used variations of the base signs.... This fact has emerged as a result of analyzing the texts that were being repeated and that have been presented on the drawing...

Secondly: the words, and in some cases whole phrases, were written with the aid of ligatures, i.e. clusters of signs. Also the way of constructing the ligatures may be reproduced by analysing the repeated texts. The ligatures were constructed in a variety of ways... once the entire base signs were clustered, or only their fragments were assembled into one, sometimes grotesque whole...

The fact that the most characteristic elements of the base signs could be connected with each other in many ways caused that one and the same word was recorded with different ligatures... The graphic variety of signs in the cult texts was multiplied by the use of rebus-like phrases, based on ambiguity of the Dravidian signs.

There were also multiplications of the same signs in the Easter Island texts—actually as in the Indus Valley texts—they resulted from the ambiguity of Dravidian numerals, or from their sonic similarity to certain cult phrases. It is illustrated below:

IRU = two = great,
TIRU, TIRI = three = holy,
NAAL, NAL = four = good.[†]

...We may also point out two further things.

Firstly: the Easter Island scripts, preserved on wooden objects, have a cult character and that probably explains why the successive copyists tried to make works of art out of them. The scripts were enriched by the generations of copyists with additional "rebuses," variants of signs and so on. All however on the basis of unchanging set of syllables and signs—those remained unchanged since the times of the Indus Valley civilization, i.e for at least 5,000 years.

The latest texts from the Island—copied already by the Polynesians only, who didn't know the sonic values of the signs, as well as the Dravidian language, are partially distorted...

It follows from my research that the Easter Island writings constitute sequences of short ritual formulas praising the avatar—incarnation or son of the god. *These texts do not contain any genealogies, historical traditions or tales.*

[Here] are some examples of these formulas's translations. The writings very often [speak] about a bird (Tamil word WII), that is named the "king, god and star." It is illustrated by the drawing. This bird is depicted by such attributes as "heavenly, merciful, fiery."..

Analysis of the repeated fragments indicates that this "merciful bird" was an avatar—which is an embodiment of a god (TOOTTAL—pronounced similarly like TOTAR/TOTAL—a chain, garland, necklace). Use of this sign's name to record the idea "appearance of a god" is illustrated by the drawing... Both the terms "bird" as well as "appearance" are associated with the word KOO = the king... The avatar was also presented as "bird-man" and "star-man." It's also worth noticing two other names of the god: MAKA MAKA and NARMINI. ...

It follows from the scripts that MAKA MAKA was "warlike" or "valiant.".. In some writings from

the Island—especially on the Santiago Stick—
many short ritual formulas occur, addressed to the
avatar and ending with the word …MIIL—"save
us!" or "rescue us!" [7]

Whew!

The mysterious bird-man figure, appearing not only as a sign of
writing, but also in the form of various reliefs and wooden statues,
is simply the symbol of the god, worshipped throughout the "3=1
empire"! But it was a symbol—not a *literal* image. Maybe it was
just about the fact that this avatar has *arrived* on Earth, i.e., that
the avatar descended from the sky? After all, he was also named
the "star-god." Some of the most common sets of hieroglyphs
represent the following formulas: "heavenly bird, merciful bird,
fiery bird, king" (mii-wii, ta-ya-wii, ti-wii koo) and "king-bird,
star-bird, god-bird" (mii-koo, wii-mii, wii-tee). In the Indus Valley
he was often presented on something resembling a polygonal,
many-sided cross and often this shape itself was considered its
symbol. Sometimes it was just a cross, as if consisting of five
squares, in other instances it was a figure more resembling a
square with "step-like" sides. It shouldn't surprise us, in light of
all the other analogies, that it's known also from the Andes (from
Tiahuanaco in particular) as the "Andean cross"! In both cases it
clearly had a religious meaning and, what is more striking, the
god's embodiment or son was usually placed in front of it.

The similarity to the Christian context is amazing, although
there is no doubt that the Indus Valley culture is a lot older than
the Christian model. Of course, it may be a coincidence, but one
should bear in mind that quite a significant part of the Bible and
the Christian religious tradition is in fact of much older origin
and constitutes a kind of "mix" of various pagan traditions and
symbols, from the "Christmas tree" through the "Easter egg,"
both ancient symbols of rebirth. Christmas replaced the winter
solstice but the old symbol remained. The Sumerian myth of the
flood and the story of Noah in Genesis, are further examples. The
whole "Our Father" prayer is a literal quotation from the Egyptian
Book of the Dead. Because in their religion each prayer had to be
followed by the name of the respective god as "an address," if you

like, there was the name "Amon" at the end, which was translated as "amen."

There is an indication that some Christian elements are in fact of Indian origin, such as the myth of the Virgin Birth and the Slaughter of the Innocents, so too the Cross as symbol of the god's son could also have come from there, earlier, and has been in fact only transformed. But there's no doubt that it may all be a coincidence as well. There is also a possibility—pure speculation this time—that the Crucifixion also took place in the Indus Valley, independently and earlier!

Professor Szalek draws a conclusion on the basis of his discoveries that it was the Tamils who brought their empire's heritage to Easter Island. But there is actually a certain problem with that... for there is undoubtedly no trace of such a migration there. Indeed, quite the contrary: according to all the reports from the first encounters, the "long-ears" certainly had a relatively bright skin (unlike the Tamils or Dravidians) and were very tall. As even professor Szalek wrote: "The anthropological studies of the old skulls from megalithic graves indicate an amazing fact, namely that around 60% of Easter Island's population *was of Europoidal origin*."[7]

Reading this, we should bear in mind that the phrase "of Europoidal origin" means in this case that they had been classified, on the basis of the anthropological data, as members of a certain anthropological type—and therefore certainly shared the roots with the people (one of the peoples, to be exact) which later migrated westward, to Europe, *but not that they came from Europe!* It is a very important distinction, for it seems simply that apart from the "classic" Europeans that we know today, there was an ethnic group which has migrated both to the west (the Finno-Ugric people referred to earlier), but also, if not mostly—eastward! And even though we pretty well know the fate of the western offshoot, it doesn't seem to be the case with their eastern colleagues.

Probably it was somehow related to the multi-ethnic character of the "3=1 empire," but in any case we have to go back, briefly, to the issue of who inhabited the Indus Valley. It is precisely the question of the Dravidians that requires certain clarification, and I'm afraid that without it the picture will be somewhat murky. To clarify this, I have to resort to another magnificent book written by Alexander Kondratov, entitled *Lemuria: A Key to the Past*. Lemuria was a continent from the time of the dinosaurs, a large island, that was located between today's India and Africa; the Seychelles islands are surviving mountain tops of this continent. Quoting from Kondratov:

> Although the British have used the bricks from Harappa[††] to construct their railway line, luckily they didn't broach the nearby old graveyard. Indian anthropologists—P. Gupta, P. Datta and H. Basu have carried out an analysis of the skulls found there. The authors claim that *most of the skulls* from the Harappa cemetery must be rated to the *Europoidal type*—with long head, lightly inclined, high forehead and protruding, narrow nose. Apart from these skulls, strongly represented was however a second type—characterized by a barely marked beard, flat and wide nose and other features typical for the so-called south-Indian local variation. This variation is also called Veddoidal, for its typical representatives are the Veddans, inhabitants of the mountainous and jungle areas of Ceylon.[†††] This type occurs presently only in southern India and Ceylon…
>
> All the data indicates that from the Paleolithic, i.e. since tens of thousands of years, India was populated by black people. The Indus Valley and the surrounding areas where the Protoindian civilization flourished, was therefore inhabited by the people with appearance that presently is reflected by the Ceylonian Veddans and some other small Indian tribes belonging to the Dravidian lingual group. We should remember however that the Dravidian languages are not their native tongues… Along with the spreading of the Dravidian languages into the Indian territory the process of mixing of the Negroidal natives and Europoidal newcomers was

taking place… It follows from this that we should introduce a distinction between the "modern" Dravidian peoples—using however languages belonging to this group, but in the anthropological respect representing a racial mix—and the *Protodravidians*, the creators of the Protoindian civilization…

It is quite probable that the Protodravidians's descendants have survived until our times somewhere in today's India, preserving in their appearance the features of their race—and in culture, their oldest beliefs and rites. Many anthropologists and ethnographers believe that it finds confirmation in the members of the Toda tribe—a small group of people living in the Nilgiri mountains in southern India.

The word "Nilgiri" means "Blue Mountains." They are located where three Indian states meet: Kerala, Tamil Nadu and Karnataka…. Numerous, although very small Dravidian tribes found refuge in these mountains. The first precise information comes from the turn of the 18th and 19th centuries when the English colonizers sent an expedition into the Nilgiri mountains, headed by W. Keith, in order to carry out topographical measurements.

For many days the expedition waded higher and higher—straight into the heart of the Blue Mountains. Through all this time it has not encountered a single man, it could seem that no living soul exists in these mountains. The greater was Keith's amazement when on some afternoon a view to a picturesque valley opened before him, in which entire buffalo herds were pastured. They were taken care of by the bearded old men with clothes resembling the togas of the ancient Romans and their appearance brought to the minds of the travelers that of biblical cowherds. In this way the "Toda land"—Todanad or Todamala—was

59

discovered. It turned out later that the Portuguese also knew a lot about this land, and that even at the beginning of the 17th century. The first Christians appeared on the Malabar Coast already in the first century A.D. and, as the legend says, were headed by the Apostle Thomas... Their descendants — as was reported to the Portuguese — after their arrival to India, were supposedly still living somewhere in the mountains. The Portuguese Catholic mission couldn't miss such an opportunity. It had suffered, however, one defeat already, for the local "Christians" turned out to be the believers of the so-called Nestorian sect — i.e. heretics. So the mission did not ignore the information and immediately sent two priests into the mountains. These envoys found the Toda tribe in the depth of the Blue Mountains, but they soon realized however that nobody here had ever heard about Saint Thomas, or about the Christian faith at all. Since all the attempts to convert the Todas failed, the Portuguese soon left them in peace that lasted for two centuries, until Keith's arrival...

The mysterious tribe from the Blue Mountains for a long time raised the understandable curiosity of anthropologists, ethnographers and linguists. The Todas differed from all their neighbors at first glance. They have large, distinctive eyes, "Roman" noses and thin lips. They are characterized also by tall height and a quite bright shade of skin, moreover there [are] a lot of brown, or even red-haired, people among them.[∞] They also have light-brown or green eyes. All these features, that are lacking among the typical inhabitants of southern India, bring the Toda closer to the southern variation of the Europoidal race.

The Toda distinguish themselves also by quite peculiar habits and religion. In one of their mourning songs we encounter a mention of "the owner of seven ships," who visited "seven kingdoms and seven kings." Where could such topics come from, in the songs of a people living deep in the interior and dealing with herding? Or perhaps it's an echo of the times when Toda was a greater nation, living over the sea, a nation of sailors, just like today's Tamils? Perhaps in their faces and traditions are preserved some traces of the Protodravidians?

Of course, there's no way of considering the Todas as the descendants of the Protoindian civilization in a straight line. Harappa and Mohenjo Daro were probably constructed by some offshoot of the Protodravidians, while the other ones were mixed with the natives in Southern India... Their language belongs to the southern subgroup of the Dravidian lingual group and is akin the most to the Tamil and Malajalam, as well as to the languages of the neighboring tribes. Apart from this, the Toda priests use however a peculiar ritual language, known as "quorjam."... A renowned archaeologist with the title of king, the Greek king Peter, who visited the Todas in the years 1939 and 1949 has noticed that some words in quorjam resemble (or are even identical) to the respective words of the Sumerian language. And so, for example "Sun" in the quorjam language is called "Utu"—i.e. exactly the same as in Sumerian, actually just like the name of the Moon god—"Sin." [35]

The ties between the Protodravidians and ancient Sumer are another matter (there were only three great civilizations at the time of the Indus Valley culture—itself, Egypt, and Sumer in today's Iraq; and they all maintained close contacts with each other). But it may also be that it was the influences of the Indus Valley civilization that were noticeable in Sumer—and not vice versa. The empire nicknamed by Professor Szalek as the "three races—one language empire" must have indeed been powerful if the influence is quite fundamental in nature. My intention is not to bore the reader with the Sumerian thread but merely to mention it, since it will emerge again in quite a crucial and amazing context in South America, so it's worth pursuing a little further.

Sumer, or Sumerian civilization, was always considered the cradle of human culture in general. It's not a coincidence that one of the basic books on it has the title *History Begins in Sumer*.[12] At the same time, however, it turns out that even the Sumerians took over the foundations of this mysterious "super-civilization" that used the Dravidian language. According to the standard view, the roots from which the Sumerian civilization grew is a so-called al-Ubaid culture, generally recognized as the oldest on Earth. It wasn't, however, anything other than a "carrier" of the Dravidian (Protodravidian) culture. The names of the oldest cities in Sumer bear the "ur" cores (for example, Ur, Uruk, Nippur, Durum, Assur, Shurupak, and so on), which in Dravidian means "city" or "hamlet." The Ubaid words defining various professions (which is some indication of the civilization's roots!) have the Dravidian suffix "gar"—meaning "the hand"—such as "engar," the peasant; "nangar," the carpenter; "damgar," the merchant; etc.

The deeper we reach into the past, therefore, the more often we realize that in fact all the old civilizations on our planet drew from one and the same source. This aspect is peppered by the fact that to this day the Sumerians' place of origin is unknown. In a book with a telling title—*The Sumerians's Forgotten World*—I have found information that according to their legends they did come *from the east*.[36]

With this in mind we may now go back to the white people from Asia. In a later part of this book I will obviously connect this "story" with the mystery of Easter Island's and will connect it even farther, to the Americas. But we will stay in Asia for a while yet, for it was a place of quite amazing discoveries in this respect in recent years.

These discoveries are stunning in that they have effectively revolutionized our understanding of human history's most remote past (or at least the scientific understanding of it). As I mentioned, before the main wave of migration to Europe, there was a very different, older migration of Protodravidian or Finno-Ugric people in Europe—but this one went not only westward, but also to the east. We will now trace back their track.

Here's a fragment of an article that appeared in one of our popular magazines, in 1997: [37]

> The white mummies constitute a real mystery. In the most remote corner of Central Asia there have been discovered corpses that look like modern Germans, Irish or Scandinavians. When almost 20 years ago, in the Chinese Sinkiang (Xinjiang) province, the first mummies of a white people were found, nobody paid attention to this discovery. The scientists from the "Land of the Middle," considering their culture as autonomous, developing itself in isolation from external influence, thought that bodies buried in the valley are remains of some wanderers or slaves from distant Europe. But as time passed, over 100 such mummies have been found.
>
> Today we know already that four thousand years ago the Tarim valley was inhabited by a people, whose members had bright red or brownish hair, blue eyes, white skin and "European" facial features. The extremely dry and hot climate has perfectly preserved the bodies of the dead. By the corpses some funeral gifts were found: sheep bones, wooden utensils. The mummies were wrapped up with wool blankets, on their feet were tall boots, on their heads—conical hats. At the body of a three-month old baby there lay a "bottle" for feeding with a dummy made of sheep's udder. The mysterious blond-haired tribe knew the wheel, used bronze objects and lived in circular huts. The ornaments and decorations on their robes display similarity to the patterns found in the Mediterranean basin and in Northern Europe.
>
> The discovery of these "European" mummies in the very heart of Asia may lead to a revolution in science. Could the Indoeuropeans reach as far

as the Tarim valley—at the edge of the Kazakh steppes, by the Mongolian border? Would they spread not only to the west, as the ethnologists claimed so far, but also to the east, reaching as far as Central China? "It's one of the most significant discoveries of this century," Vincent Pigott from the Pennsylvania State University doesn't hide his enthusiasm. The scientists are waging a fierce contention whether similar cultures in various parts of the world developed independently, or perhaps share a common beginning. The Tarim valley mummies testify rather for the latter hypothesis. Their knowledge of bronze smelting may serve as an example of this—an alloy of copper and tin. According to some scientists, humans had not mastered this ability independently from each other in various places, but it was developed 4000 years ago in south-western Asia. Only from there it spread along the trade routes to the east and west. "This theory always had a gap, inside. Today we have filled it up, because thanks to the discoveries of the white mummies we know that bronze was known also in Central Asia," says American scientist Victor Mair. [37]

A very interesting article on this thread has been published on the Internet, by the American Franklin Institute. I quote certain fragments of it:

Four thousand years ago a community lived in the Tarim Basin—in what is now the Xinjiang Uygur Autonomous Region of China—in the heart of Asia. The Tarim Basin people thrived there *for at least 1500 years*. There are indications that they survived as a culture even into the second century. Then they disappeared.

Now their remains are being reclaimed from the sands and the people of that extinct nation are challenging scientists and scholars to fathom who they may have been, and—if an answer can be found—where, in prehistory, they came from. According to sweeping physical evidence, they were not Chinese. They were not even Asian. They were Causasian.°°°

For Victor Mair, a specialist in Chinese language and literature at the University of Pennsylvania, the naturally mummified bodies unearthed in the basin's Taklimakan Desert have become a passion.

"The question is whether these people were there for long, long time, or whether they migrated in from somewhere else," he said. Where did they come from, and why? ...

Learning who the Tarim Basin's inhabitants might have been, he said, is "very important for writing Asian history, and world history. In my opinion, without that region, there would be no Asian history."

For the last two years Mair has been organizing an international conference on the Tarim Basin people... "I think it's premature to draw hard-and-fast conclusions as to who these people were, and what language they spoke...," Mair said. ...Still, Mair—who saw the original collection of mummified corpses in 1987, at the region's provincial museum—will never forget his own haunting first impression of them. The bodies, recovered from graveyards long overblown with sand, were exceptionally preserved by the dry climate and the salt deposits in which they had been buried. "I was thunderstruck... I just stood there for a couple of hours. I almost thought it was some kind of hoax," he said. "All of their bodies were completely intact. *They just looked so alive.*"°°°°°

And with features so stunningly non-Asian.

They were clearly the remains of a Caucasoid people, with dark blond or yellowish hair, deep-set eyes and long limbs. Among the corpses Mair saw that day were the mummies of a man and woman from a joint grave and an infant that had been buried nearby. All three had been discovered about 10 years earlier, by Kamberi and his colleagues. "So far, 100 bodies have been excavated...," Kamberi said. "I believe that in the next 100 years the land of Central Asia will become an archaeologist's dream land..."..

"What I'm not going to do is say what I think," Mair said of the three-day conference, which will include ancient-textile specialists and linguists as well as genetic specialists and scholars. "I consciously sought out people who have differing opinions. I don't want any gospel statements," he said. That attitude is probably the safest Mair could adopt: the ancient nation of the Tarim Basin is wrapped as much in controversy as it is in mystery...
In an article Mair wrote for Archaeology magazine last year, he himself says: "The new finds are also forcing a reexamination of old Chinese books that describe historical or legendary figures of great height, with deep-set blue or green eyes, long noses, full beards, and red or blond hair. Scholars have traditionally scoffed at these accounts, but it now seems that they may be accurate." [38]

I have emphasized the "red hair," because of the similarity to the "long-eared" from the Easter Island. Recently I also found an interesting bit of information: one of these mummies, known as Yingpan Man, is 6'6" tall (1.98 m) — you can compare it with the descriptions of the Todas from India and the "long—eared."
These findings from Central China have been described, in *Archaeology* magazine, in the March/April issue from 1995, as well as in a magnificent book entitled *The Tarim Mummies*.[39] Its authors share the view that this "strange" people, although Europoidal — there can be do doubt about it — came not from *Europe*, but from southwest *Asia*. And this, of course, coincides

with the Indus Valley.

According to all the evidence, they migrated further eastward, and among others the oldest inhabitants of the Japanese islands — the Ainu — were their descendants.

(Footnotes)

* "Glotto-chronological": i.e., the "timing" of the linguistic diversification.

** 7000 B.C. is almost 9,000 years ago.

*** This discovery was made at Mohenjo Daro by the Soviet Academy of Science.

† Quite a strange language!

†† The second important city of the Indus Valley.

††† Now Sri Lanka

∞ The long-eared people from Easter Island were also, let it be recalled, red- or brown-haired, and tall.

∞∞ Europoids, which doesn't mean—I repeat—that they had come from Europe

∞∞∞ Thousands of years old!!!

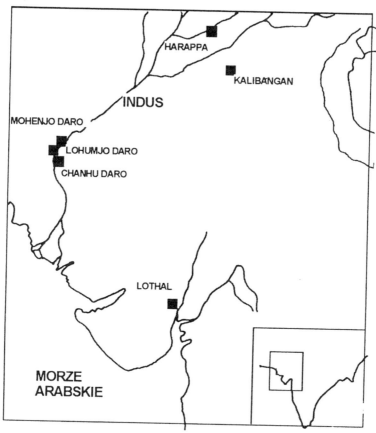

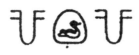

Top: Map of Indus Valley cities.

Left: Various representations of the bird – embodiment of the god (avatar) from the Indus Valley culture. The symbol on top was the most often used. It's the multi-stepped cross, identical with the so-called Andean cross whose function was as the same at Tiahuanaco. Note that the bottom variant portrays something looking like a disc-bird hybrid, as in Sumer (B. Z. Szalek, with author's permission).

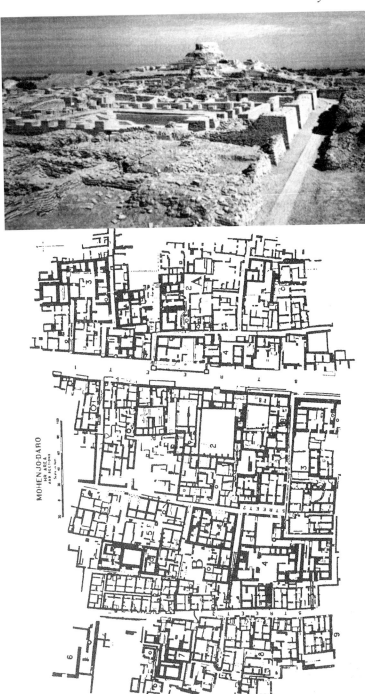

Top: The citadel at Mohenjo Daro. Bottom: A map of the city.

Photo of skeletons excavated in the streets of Mohenjo Daro. The haphazard positions in which they lie, and the fact that there was apparently no one left to bury the dead, speak to suddenness of the doom that descended here.

Example from the Rong Rongo writing of Easter Island – two records of the same prayer, in which the noted signs are interchangeabile (B. Z. Szalek, with author's permission).

Sign	Syllable	Sign	Syllable	Sign	Syllable
Ƴ, Ý	KA	⌐	TU	◇	YEE
☆	KAA	�	TE	ℑ	LI=RI
ℬ, ☖	KI	☖	TEE	E	WA
α	KU	ℰ, ☷, ⊞	TO	⋔ρ	WAA
∧	KUU	⫶⫶	PA	ℬ, ☆θ	WI
⪡	KOO	曲	PAA	⋏	
♭	SA	ℰ	PE/PI	ℚ	WII
✖	SAA	⊥, ⊔	PU?	U	WU
⌂	SI	ψ	MA	Γ	WUU?
⋈	SU	⚱	MAA	⫶⫶	WEE
∩	SE	⅄, ⊙	MII	⫶⫶	WE
⚠	NA	⚲	MU	∣	WO
⫼	NAA	⫶⫶	MUU	⟨	WOO?
⊞, ⊡	NU	⅄	YA	⫼⫼	CAY
✶, ⅄	TA	大	YAA	⫶⫶	CA
△	TAA	‖	YI		
∞, ⋴	TI	⊗	YÜ?		

Top: Professor Szalek's decoding of the signs and symbols found in Indus Valley writing.

Left: Professor Szalek showing his diagram of the "Axis of the World."

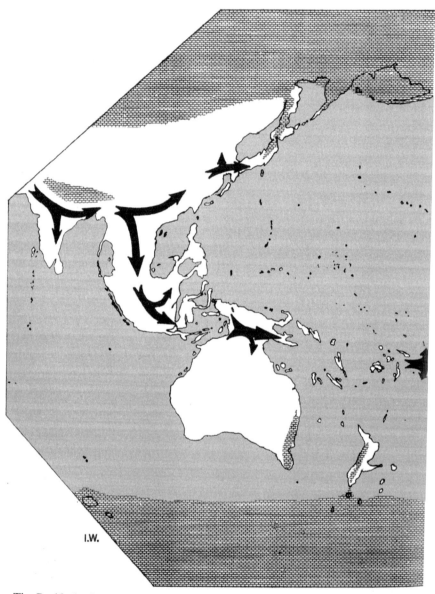

The Pacific basin – the shaded areas reflect the range of the glaciers; the arrows mark possible routes of migrations (I. Witkowski).

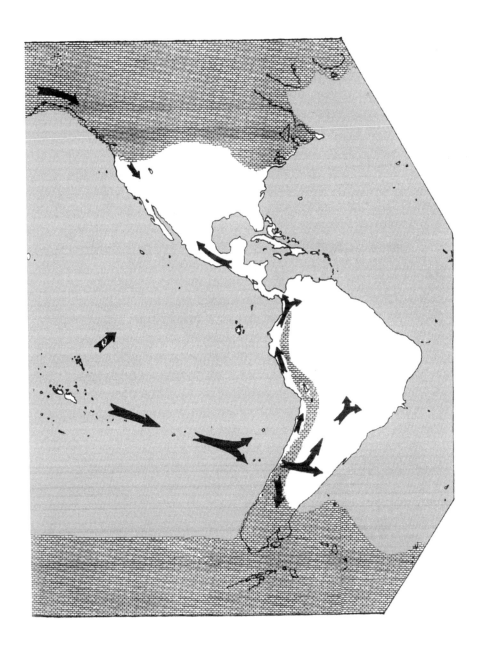

Top: Two views of a bust of one of the "Priest Kings" of the Indus Valley culture. Bottom: A view of the streets and gutters of Mohenjo Daro.

3

HYPOTHESES—COULD THERE BE A LOST LAND IN THE PACIFIC?

As we can see from the content of the previous chapter, there are various tracks left by the "Protodravidians," one leading to Europe, and the other to Japan via China. But the most interesting one is the one leading straight to Easter Island. After all, the geometrical "Axis" (Mohenjo Daro—Nan Madol—Easter Island) is a clear indication left for future generations that we should look closer in that exact direction.

There is a clear track left in the Pacific, in the form of various, sometimes strange cultures, but there are also "civilizational" traces—There are similarities in the traditions of certain islands, as well as other places where the Rongo Rongo writing was found, oftentimes quite far away from the main route. As Professor Szalek states in his publication:

> It is known that in 1851, in the home of a Maori chief in New Zealand, a wooden breastplate (Rei miro) was found, 41 cm long, covered by signs known from the Easter Island. Dr J. Huppertz indicates, in his book on the Island, an interesting bit of information, published by J. Park Harrison in his book from 1874 entitled Note on Easter Island Writing. He wrote that the New Zealand chiefs recognized the Rongo Rongo writing as something that they used themselves, in the past."
> And:
> "In 1974 L. Rollin reported that signs resembling the Rongo Rongo have been found on the Marquesas Islands."

I will take this occasion to quote Professor Szalek's description that pertains to the same kind of writing that was found in *Europe*, which only bears testimony as to the scale of influence — global — that the empire exerted in various parts of the world: [7]

> During his visit in Szczecin Professor E. Wiebeck pointed out a greatly peculiar and ancient artifact that has provoked the consternation of some researchers for 30 years. It concerned two golden horns, found in the years 1639 and 1743. The horn that was accidentally found lying in the ground, in 1639, weighted around 3 kg* and was 68 cm long.** The first of the horn's segments, looking from the thicker end, lacked any drawings. The other segment was however covered with two lines of signs...
>
> The golden horns became property of the king of Denmark. In 1802 they were stolen and melted — but luckily before that castings were made (and copies after that), as well as exact reproductions of the signs. The golden copies have been placed in a museum in Copenhagen...
>
> Professor Wiebeck asked me a question: could it be proven that the inscription on one of these horns was made with Easter Island writing? So I began comparative studies of the horn's inscription and the Easter Island writings. I have come to the conclusion that apart from similarity of the specific signs, we are dealing with multiple analogies here... It proves that the inscription was made with the Tamil (=Dravidian) writing, known from the Easter Island. Well — we could say — that fact constitutes no revelation. But the facts will become mysterious if we'll take the place where the golden horn was found into the account — it was in the Danish village of Gallehus, in 1639... The horns are dated to 400 A.D., while Easter Island was visited by the Dutch admiral Roggeveen as late as in 1722. [7]

With this in mind, we return to the subject of the "eastern" migration and to the Pacific.

Just as in Asia, clear traces of an old migration can be found on this ocean's countless islands and archipelagos. The situation resembles the problem that science had with the Dravidians/Protodravidians, only this time the difficulty consists of the fact that it is rather difficult to reach deep enough to identify the migration which preceded the Polynesians—but we will come back to this, briefly, later.

For the time being let's just consider the option that, a long time ago, there existed in the Pacific some "lost continent." I probably wouldn't try to check this track if it were not for the fact that numerous Polynesian legends (including the one from Easter Island which appeared earlier in the book) speak about some sunken land, from which the first migrants had to flee. It's a notion suspiciously vivid in the legends throughout the Pacific. By the way—in one of Kondratov's books I found an interesting piece of information: in the treasure trove of another great civilization, namely the Egyptian, there is a clear mention (on an original scroll that has been translated) that once there was a great land in the east, among the waters of "Uaj-ur" (as they named the eastern seas) that has been claimed by the sea.

So, lets take a closer look at this.

It was as early as the 1860's when the topic of the existence of "lost continents" began to be discussed among geologists and geographers. The fact that raised their interest was that there are certain similarities between various distant lands, islands and continents. Initially this discussion referred mostly to the similarities in flora and fauna between India and Southern Africa. The geologists tossed in their bit (mostly the British geologist William T. Blanford), noticing that in certain strata, mostly from the Permian period, the composition and thickness of various layers match each other quite precisely, as if in that period they were lying on the same piece of land that was torn apart due to tectonic processes. Blanford proposed the theory that the Permian epoch there was a "land bridge" connecting the south of Africa with the Indian subcontinent. Supposedly it comprised today's islands of Madagascar, the Seychelles, Maldives and Laccadives. As I mentioned previously, the islands from this "sector" of the Indian Ocean distinguish themselves from other, similar islands in that they are not built on coral reefs or volcanic cones, but consist of solid rock, resembling a continental plate. The trouble was, of course, that they're in the middle (or almost the middle) of the ocean. In 1887 an Austrian paleontologist named Neumayer published the first paleontological map of the world portraying the continents as they supposedly looked in the "reptile era," that is, in the Jurrasic period, to employ the modern terminology. He placed there a strangely named "Brazilian-Ethiopian land mass." The theory itself, although modified and dissecteds, somehow stood the test of time and was generally accepted. This impelled the scientists to formulate further hypotheses.

These were picked up by the naturalists and evolutionists, who then used them to explain some unusual cases of plants' and animals' radiation to various, distant places on our planet. The German biologist and evolutionist Ernst Haeckel formulated a theory pertaining to the radiation and evolution of lemurs in the Indian Ocean's basin that turned out to be quite accurate, successful, and therefore, popular. It should be pointed out that back then the interest in science on the part of the populace was far greater than today, probably thanks to the fact that it was much easier to grasp for the general public. For the first time in history science had managed to revolutionize the perception of the world in several respects; people found out about the variety of nature, of past civilizations, etc. Haeckel's theory contributed to the popularity of the word "Lemuria," the lost continent that once existed east of Africa. As is often the case, the "blowback" of the aforementioned popularity was that scientific theories, and this one in particular, were misunderstood and to some extent corrupted by maniacs. I refer to the case of the Russian Helena Pietrovna Blavatska, who established the Theosophical Society and successfully promoted the "Lemuria" theory, only in her version it supposedly existed in the *Pacific*. Some obscure "sources," such as contacts with ghosts, gave her a basis to construct a self-consistent, quasi-religious vision of a land of plenty, divine social and moral order, and ancient "wise men." These theories gave rise to countless popular novels, comic books and so on, and were generally renowned, although for obvious reasons they didn't contribute anything that would enable any progress in understanding and real knowledge. As a consequence, for some time the notion of lost continents died.

Its revival came after Alfred Wegener formulated a comprehensive theory of continental drift. That was in 1912, but only after World War II did it spread to the scientific world for good. Shortly after that a theory of "Gondwana" was postulated and it's still very much acknowledged. "Gondwana" was supposedly a "super continent," a single world mega-island, from which other continents separated in various periods. But contrary to the generally accepted viewpoint, Wegener wasn't the inventor of the idea that once the continents were connected with each other.

A map displaying the mega-continent, that was about to break down, was drawn for the first time by the brilliant Russian scholar, Mikhail Lomonosov, as early as 1763. One has to admit that he was a scientist not only gifted with brilliant intuition, but also thoroughly educated as a naturalist, chemist, philologist, philosopher, the creator of two schools of poetry, and a member of three academies of science. A draft of this continent that was supposed to exist "before the deluge" (there was no such idea as geological timing then) turned out later to be fairly accurate. The only problem that became apparent was that, as Lomonosov himself admitted, he made the map on the basis of some "very old maps from ancient times"! Sounds like a fairy tale, but I found this information in a popular scientific book titled *The Origin and Structure of the Continents,* published in Poland in 1970. The first scientific dissertation more or less comprehensively approaching the subject on the basis of Wegener's theory was published as late as 1954. It was the book titled *The Lost Continents*, by L. Sprague de Camp, better known as the author of some of the "Conan" stories, but a good scholar too.

Earlier—in the interwar period—a whole series of popular books was published that referred to the lost continent in the Pacific. Their author was the renowned James Churchward and he named the continent "Mu." What they contained wasn't an analysis of facts, but rather more or less mystical digressions; nevertheless they were sometimes quite interesting. According to Churchward, he had been shown a "hidden library" in Tibet or India, the content of which provided his inspiration. In all probability it was just a trick aimed to publicize the whole commercial effort, but it in turn was probably inspired by quite a lot of earlier reports and tales that stated that such hidden libraries indeed existed and that they hid some knowledge about our remote past.

These reports were based mostly on the story of a British traveler, Sir Aurel Stein from the first decade of the twentieth century. In 1907 he reached just such a library hidden in a cave near a Dunhuang village, which had been discovered in 1900 by a Tibetan monk. It contained hundreds of very old manuscripts. Such "caches" were dug out in earlier epochs quite routinely in order to secure the priceless records copied by the monks, and to save them from burning by savage hordes, like the Mongols. Aurel Stein claimed that he saw books and scrolls written in Chinese, in Sanskrit (Tibetan writing), but also in languages or with hieroglyphs he had never seen before. And it was precisely he who contributed to "Mu's" popularity. He claimed that among the scrolls uncovered in 1900, there was also an incomplete ancient map portraying the lost continent in the middle of the Pacific Ocean.

In the many publications that were the inevitable outgrowth of such claims, the thread was being gradually developed and the longer it went on, the more utopian the Pacific land became. Eventually, all the followers agreed that there was a high civilization, ruled by some "divine beings" or a "higher race" that caused that the land to be like a "lighthouse" or a magic "lantern," enlightening the entire world and the surrounding continents by the power of its moral and scientific superiority.

Perhaps, like every legend, it was rooted in fact in some remote, actual event. In any case, it is undoubtedly true in the legends from the Pacific, as we know from the example of the Easter Islanders. Even in the Americas there are similar legends in which the development of human civilization started on the same or similar "lost land." In 1979 a German NASA scientist, Josef Blumrich, published in Germany a book (*Kaskara und die sieben Welten**** on the Hopi Indians' legends which contain such a thread. The Hopi chief, a very educated man by the way, tells the main legend of his people there, according to which their motherland was sinking and its inhabitants were evacuated to South America, to Tiahuanaco! Later on they supposedly started the march northwards from there, eventually reaching North America. As in the case of Polynesian legends, it was a continent—or just a large land—where people lived mlong the gods or god-like creatures (recall once again the Easter Island legends where Make Make was a living, material being). In the case of the Hopi Indians, they were called the Kachinas, which means "the estimable beings possessing knowledge of development." The name "Kachina" is a derivative of the word "development." The lost continent was in turn called "Kaskara," which was a large island in the equatorial zone of the Pacific. By the way: such striking similarities between the Polynesian and Indian traditions once again testify for the theory linking these two "worlds" through a common migration.

This same motif of a lost continent emanates from the version popularized by Churchward, supposedly based on some previously hidden Tibetan manuscripts. If we consider Tibet as one of the "offshoots" of that ancient civilization, then it's worth taking into account that it also fits the scheme of similarities with Easter Island and—farther on—with South America. The entire custom or feature tied with long ears as a benchmark of the rulers/wise masters is quite evident on the Indian subcontinent and also in Tibet. Buddha, as well as their equivalents of the saints, the Bhodisattvas, are generally portrayed with elongated. One of the strangest discoveries leading us to Tibet is that according to the newest linguistic studies by the American scientist E. Sapir and others, there is a group of Indian languages known as the Na-Dene, used among others by the Navajo tribe, which display clear similarities to the so-called Tibeto-Burman languages used in Tibet and India.[14]

Now, when we know the historic background, we may ask ourselves a question: what does the question of such lands' possible existence—or more generally, the existence of sunken lands in the Pacific—look like in the light of modern scientific knowledge?

There are various theories that apply here in some respect.

Many geologists wondered, for example, how it was possible for the "super-continent" of Gondwana (from the time of the dinosaurs) to exist without some kind of counterbalance on the other side, i.e. in what is presently the Pacific Ocean. It's hard to imagine that for some reason all the land masses mounted a "plot" to assemble on one side of our planet, leaving the "surprised waters" alone on the other side. That's just not possible. There must have been something!

Once the hypothesis has been postulated that such a continent still exists, that is, that it hasn't collapsed into the abyss, then it is apparent what it is: the Moon (see for example J. Darwin, H. Quiring). As time passed and lunar geology developed (logically, it should be "lunology") such a possibility was ruled out. But in light of the Pacific basin's still unclear geology, we cannot rule out that such a land existed even after Gondwana broke into pieces. In the book, which I mentioned earlier, on the origin of the continents, I found the following bit of information, significant from our point of view:

> The fact why this primordial ocean lives to this day in the most turbulent tectonic life remains a mystery; why it is entirely surrounded by a zone of young volcanic activity, seismic and volcanic phenomena. The Pacific's bottom displays a significant mobility, which is evidenced by the changes in the development of coral reefs, covering the underwater slopes of the islands.

As author Vincent Gaddis states in his book entitled *Invisible Horizons*, instances are known of the real disappearance of islands in the Pacific.

The English pirate Edward Davis discovered, in 1687, a huge—as he described it—island. It supposedly had a "long, sandy beach with coconut palms" and land allegedly spreading to the horizon. He noted the location: 27°S and around 500 miles to the west off the coast of South America, which coincides with the location of the known Desventurados archipelago, consisting of small islands, being the mountain tops of a large, underwater ridge called Juan Fernandez. However, no such a large island—"Davis land"—was ever found there.

82

In more recent times, in 1802, another peculiar case occurred, quite close to Easter Island, as if it had not enough mysteries of its own! This time it was another Englishman, Captain Gwyn, who spotted a medium-sized, rocky island some 300 miles to the west off Easter Island's coast and 50 miles to the south. He came to the conclusion that because it wasn't on the map, it must have been the Sala y Gomez island, in fact located around 200 miles to the northeast off Easter Island, and that some cartographer just put it on the map in the wrong place. This "mistake" was visible, however, on other maps as well, and the location turned out to be correct. Gwyn's strange observation should then be considered a *fata-morgana* at best, but the trouble is that another sailor, in 1879 also noted that he saw apparently the same island, in that "impossible" place. This time it was an Italian, who marked a "new" island in exactly the same location and named it after his own ship, *Podesta*. This discovery was officially acknowledged and such an island was from then on printed on other maps; only in 1935 it was officially considered a "ghost," bringing to mind the legend from Easter Island in which the locals stated that some time ago their land was somewhat bigger.

But that's not all! In 1932, and therefore quite recently, the vessels of the US Pacific Fleet unsuccessfully tried to find an island named Sarah Ann, which on their maps also existed close to Easter Island. There was a whole expedition heading there that was about to prepare some field observatory for the expected total eclipse of the Sun, for it was the best location. The search lasted several weeks, after which the Admiralty had to admit that there was no such island.

I have emphasized the reports referring to the southeastern Pacific because they seem to be the most intriguing, but there is a lot more to it, such as the "nonexistent" islands of Marquenn, Sprague, Favorite, Monks, Dangerous, Duke of York, Grand Duke, Alexander, Little Paternosters, Massacre, Mortlock, and St. Vincent; and even this list is incomplete.

Of course it may just involve misunderstandings, misinterpretations and a whole chain of coincidences, but generally I think that we should bear these facts in mind.

So we see, the possibility that there was a large, "lost"

landmass in the Pacific isn't as weird as it might have seemed at first glance. I quote below fragments of an article written by geologists, which has been published in a very serious scientific magazine—in *Nature*. It bears the title—nomen omen—"The Lost Pacifica Continent":

> Major wide mountain belts exist, morphologically similar to the Alpine belt, in regions which do not experience continental collisions, such as western North America, Alaska, east Siberia and the Andes. The crustal thickness here can also be very great, up to 70 km in the Andes. All are seismically active, wide, highly deformed and include high plateaus of various sizes. Many of these wide orogenic rocks also exhibit great geological complexities which are not simply explained by the model of an oceanic lithosphere under-thrusting a continental lithosphere. We suggest therefore, that the circum Pacific mountain belts may be the result of past continental collisions, similar to those associated with the Alpine belt...
>
> Hamilton has proposed that Permian terrains bearing Tethyan fusulinids may be formed *in the central Pacific on island arcs*, which were subsequently swept into the North American continent. Furthermore, these North American terrains share Jurrasic and Cretaceous faunas and floras with New Zealand, [New] Caledonia, the Antarctic peninsula and Chile. This is consistent with several palaeomagnetic studies, which suggest that large fragments in the western USA, Canada and in Alaska were located near the equator, perhaps in the Triassic times. Hillhouse found that tholeiitic flows in the Wrangell mountain area were formed 15° north or south of the equator during the Triassic time...
>
> In Central and South America there are numerous old basement inclusions within the

mobile belts, some of which extend well into the Pacific Ocean itself—suggesting past continental collisions. During the Jurassic, South America was bound to the west by volcanic rocks resting on strongly folded and metamorphosed rocks off Patagonia, Ecuador, Peru and Bolivia…

The situation is perhaps best summarised by James: Jurassic volcanic rocks in southern Peru are wedged in among crystalline metamorphic rocks at least 400 million years old. What these remnants of ancient sialic crust are doing some 300 km west of the currently exposed geosynclinal rocks of the continental margin is unknown. These rocks could be part of the palaeozoic *microcontinent that lay to the west of the South American coastline…*

Ancient rocks reappear west of the Bering Sea along the north-west rim of the Pacific, where similar terrains of Palaeozoic age occur in north-east USSR, in Japan and discontinuously further south along the west Pacific rim. Thus not unlike North America and the Andes, mysterious continental masses in the Pacific have been involved in East Siberia, China and Japan. Many of these bodies bear strong evidence for continental origins as indicated by the nature of the old rocks exposed.

We propose that these chunks were parts of a continental mass which has disaggregated, perhaps the way Gondwana has and Africa is and may continue to disaggregate…

We call this mass "Pacifica"—to emphasize its centrality in the Pacific geological history…

Before its breakup Pacifica could have been somewhere in the neighbourhood of Australia… In fact, the concept of Pacifica was first introduced by biogeographers solely to explain the relation between the species and families surrounding the Pacific. Our results may, therefore, provide the geophysical and geological detail necessary to understand the continental and biological history in the Pacific. We believe that the combined evidence from geophysics, geology and biology makes a compelling case for a now extinct Pacifica continent, whose fragmented remains are mostly now embedded in the circum Pacific mountain belts. [40]

So, the existence of such a large land in the remote past is not merely a fantasy.

Unfortunately however, on the basis of the tectonic theories, its existence can only be spoken of in reference to the *remote past*. According to the hypothesis presented by the authors of the above article, and those to which they referred, it's from the Jurassic period, the time when dinosaurs ruled on Earth. It would be a long time before mammals took a significant position in the animal world, let alone humans. The gap between this time scale and the scale imposed by the "human history" and the expansion of our species is so enormous (by a factor of 1000 at least!) that it absolutely rules out that the processes are somehow tied to each other.

How then could a "lost land" exist in much more recent times? Is it possible at all?

In my view, despite the apparent contradiction, the existence of "lost lands" in the Pacific is not only possible, but one can even say that it's certain. How?

Simply by recognizing that tectonic processes are not the only ones which may contribute to a lost continent here. In the time scale relevant in this respect (tens of thousands of years), the dominating processes that affect the size of lands are climatic changes, and glaciations in particular. Presently we live in a quite warm (interglacial) period—in all probability just between two ice ages, which for some unclear reason haunt us periodically, scientists believe roughly every 100.000 years. To put it frankly, nobody knows why for sure—the most often encountered explanation is that our Sun "works" irregularly and displays periods of intensified or diminished activity; but this hardly finds confirmation in the form of observation of other stars, for astronomy is too young to study such long periods. There is also a hypothesis that ice ages are caused when our planetary system passes through some dust clouds or periodic density waves in our galaxy's spiral arm, in which we live. The dust would block the Sun's light and therefore cause "global cooling." But never mind all this. We will not solve this question anyway.

What *is* important is that ice ages do happen, and that the last one ended more or less 11000-12000 years ago. The estimates vary as to how much colder it really was, but on average they speak about a difference the order of over 10°C, or around 20°F. That's quite a lot and obviously it led to the accumulation of a huge mass of water in the form of polar ice caps. Presently the glaciers occupy an area of 15 million km^2 (5.8 million sq. miles). According to estimates, as well as measurements in the terrain, in the maximum of the last glaciation it was an area of around 50 million km^2, hence over three times larger. This seriously affected the maritime landscapes by uncovering large masses of land that previously were hidden under the waves.

Traces of the old coastlines are still more or less clearly visible and they contribute to the picture, according to which 20,000 years ago the sea level was 120-150 m lower (340-490 ft.). In the slightly colder period between 22 and 72 thousand years ago this drop amounted on average, on the world scale, to around 300 meters (1000 ft.). If we add to this the very small but measurable changes caused by the tectonic uplifting/sinking of lands, we get quite reasonable values. As we know, the bottom of the Pacific sinks at a steady pace, at the expense of the upheaval of the mountain ridges in the Pacific Rim.

Recently, scientists from the University of Chicago carried out radiocarbon dating of the shells deposited by mollusks on the Peruvian shore of the ocean and it has shown that during the last 5000 years this shore has been uplifted on average by 20 m (65 feet). The rate could, however, be different in various geological periods and it's not certain how it translates into the sinking of lands in the ocean's center itself.

This case is by no means new. It was Charles Darwin who first pointed out the occurrence of relatively young marine fossils, even in the high parts of the Andes, after his voyage around

South America on the *Beagle* (1831-1835). It has triggered broad contention in the scientific world, and although he managed to "plant" certain ideas, generally he met with opposition from academics. At the time, certainly, less was known about geology that might prove the correctness of such theories.

If we then assume for example a period of 50,000 years, then we'll get a change caused by tectonic sinking on the order of up to 200 meters and a "glacial" change on the order of 200-300 meters, which leads to the conclusion that certain portions of land in the central Pacific could then have been some 400-500 meters higher than at present (1300-1600 feet). If we look at the map of this ocean, we will see that this is a value sufficient to alter the picture of the archipelagos quite significantly. First and foremost, it's plain to see that the countless small islands, located often very close to each other, once were merged together forming single land masses.

As we see, not only could the "Bering land bridge" (or Beringia, the present bottom of the Bering Sea dividing Alaska and Siberia, over which the first Indians supposedly entered the North American continent) rise out of the abyss, but also quite a lot of entirely new lands become available as stepping-stones for some possible seafarers from Asia. The Indo-Chinese peninsula (Vietnam, Cambodia and so on) grows to such an extent that it absorbs large parts of the present Indonesia, Philippines and New Guinea, and nears Australia. Some quite large islands existed in the central Pacific, further on, consisting of "enlarged" versions of present-day archipelagos such as the Marquesas, Tuamotu and the Society Islands. The combined area of land probably was comparable to, or even larger than New Zealand now. Only around a 1000 miles (or 1600 kilometers) of sea divided it from Easter Island. It was really nothing, no more than a week of sailing.

In all, it turns out that the Pacific Ocean, was during the last glaciation, smaller than it is today. Perhaps it isn't such a stupid idea to consider this route as relatively easy for the voyagers of that time—if not the easiest! After all, the land bridge in the far north was a "bridge" only by name. It was an icy land resembling today's Antarctica, and went for thousands of miles—from present North Korea up to the State of Wisconsin (the middle of North

America), thus covering the distance of as much as 4000 miles at least (assuming that they would be heading straight to the target).

Imagine: you have just a sledge, probably of the kind that the present natives in the far north use (but that's an optimistic variant) and you are setting off on a journey that you almost certainly will never finish during your lifetime, nor will your grandchildren, straight into the Arctic, in the middle of the worst Ice Age. Would you do that? But that's just a reflection. What I would like to point out is that the travel through the islands wasn't as impossible as the archaeologists and anthropologists generally think, probably it was the easier alternative.

But that's a thread almost unexplored by science. And that in itself is strange, for the simple reason that in the myths of the Pacific peoples, there is a clear memory of a deluge (the end of the Ice Age?), of the sinking of large lands and even of glaciers' downright melting. For example part of the Yamana Indians's cosmogony—from the tropics!—contains just such a tale: "Lexuwakipa, which was very touchy, was feeling insulted by the people. To revenge, she allowed for a great amount of snow to fall. So much, that a great mass of ice covered the entire Earth. When eventually the ice started to melt, there was so much water that the land was completely flooded." [15]

There's no doubt that this opens entirely new possibilities, but there is also a "catch": it allows us to admit the possibility that the origins of the oldest civilizations in the Americas might have been completely different from the textbooks say, and that their roots could be a lot older, namely because the "Pacific track" contains telling evidence that the migrants brought the civilization's heritage with them, just as they brought the ready and developed Rongo Rongo script from Asia to Easter Island. That's of course a truth that cannot be accepted by conventionally-minded scholars.

Another suggestion that this might have been so, emerging also from various myths, is that there is no shortage of legends pertaining to various sunken cities—and not just in thc Pacific basin or southern Asia, but even as far north as Japan. A British researcher, Graham Hancock, has written a book dedicated entirely to this issue, entitled *Underworld*. It numbers over 700 pages!

The myths referring to a deluge or some kind of flood are by no means restricted to the Christian cultural circle, they can be found almost everywhere in the world. In fact, the biblical version is without doubt of Sumerian origin. Noah was originally the Sumerian king Ziusudra, and at the time when this part of Bible was written the Sumerian empire had been covered by desert sands for over 2000 years. If we'll recall that this people migrated to the present Iraq "from the east," through the sea, then we will inevitably face the possibility that the Pacific, the South American, and the biblical descriptions have a single source referring to one and the same sunken land; and let it be noted that no significant part of the Middle East was ever permanently flooded, apart from the regular floods caused by main rivers, which occurred every year and therefore were hardly surprising.

It's strange, by the way, that a trace of such a distant event was apparently somehow preserved in the collective memory for over ten thousand years. It's strange, but it's possible. Let me cite a couple of examples.

In many old myths there occurs a common motif of unclear origin: "beyond seven mountains, beyond seven seas." Before the first Sumerian ruins were excavated, at the turn of the 19th to the 20th century, the existence of such an ancient kingdom was only the subject of legend, much like the Trojan kingdom before it was discovered by Heinrich Schliemann (although the Bible mentioned a "Sinear kingdom" somewhere in the east). After the Sumerian cuneiform writing was decoded, the world learned that there were entire *libraries* covered by desert sand. It was discovered that among others, the aforementioned phrase was in fact Sumerian, quite commonly used and, as it turned out, it had survived for *millenia*, unchanged, mostly in verbal tradition.

Another example: an equally common motif in the myths of all the continents pertains to so-called giants, who coexisted with modern humans, but were generally hostile, and occasionally both species fought with each other for dominance. They supposedly looked like humans, only they were more powerful and hostile. However strange it seems, the giants really existed on Earth, only certainly no *later* than some 10-20 thousand years ago. In all probability, they were the members of another human species that for some time lived alongside homo sapiens: *homo erectus*.

90

One scientist, Professor Godlewski, carried out excavations of *homo erectus'* remains in Indonesia, where according to him the species survived until the end of the last glaciation. They were, in some cases, even taller than 2.5 meters, or over 8 feet (Godlewski claimed that some were up to 3 meters tall), although their brains were smaller than ours. The November 1985 issue of *National Geographic* contains an article in which the discovery of a child's skeleton is described, belonging to an 11- or 12-year old *homo erectus* which measured 1.65 meters, or almost five and a half feet. When one takes into account, from evolutionary perspective, that children in ancient times were generally smaller than today, then one can imagine a "giant," generally around 50% taller then "normal" people, a giant who undoubtedly didn't look as nice as members of the *homo sapiens*, and probably had no reason to be nice.

This, too, is strange, in that it evokes the question of how it is possible for such distant "records" to be preserved in the collective memory of very different societies. Perhaps it's a mechanism differing from normal memory. If we look, for example, at how boys play, at the ages of 3to 6, we will notice that in fact they replay some schemes from remote past, that are identical with the play of young apes: using a stick as a weapon, chasing to catch, swinging on a rope or branch, building a nest in a tree (for an ape the ability to build a nest in a tree is a fundamental condition of surviving the night), and so on. All these patterns of behavior are no longer useful in our modern world. It's a clear suggestion that "collective memories" from a very distant past are encoded, in some way, probably in DNA. So, perhaps DNA is not 85% blank, as the scientists believe, but it contains information of a different kind from that which the researchers expect to find. Perhaps not only memories from the "Ice Age," but even the memory of some "Golden Age" is also encoded, and some day we will be able to "extract" such data. But this is all obviously just reflective speculation, merely science-fiction.

We return to the main topic—to the traces of a lost civilization. There are ruins in the Pacific that are partially submerged; there is even a tale about a road that continues underwater from Easter Island. This pertains first and foremost to the mysterious Nan

Madol, the "milestone," which has been described previously. Part of this city simply lies on the ocean's bottom.

But there are not only legends and ruins that testify that once the sea level was much lower. There are also the so-called "gujots," a phenomenon characteristic of the Pacific Ocean. This French word refers to the islands from the ice age. Just as today, there were once whole archipelagos built around coral reefs, and just like today's atolls, they were completely flat. Gujots are the underwater hills or mountains that are also flat, like tables, and they all share one common feature: their "tops" are at the same depth, reflecting the ancient sea level (the depth differs, depending on which continental plate they are located on, but generally it's between 300 and 500 meters under the surface). It tells us also that the "flood" was something quick on the geological scale, and that the coral reefs' growth couldn't match that speed, for they usually grow at a rate of 1-4 meters per century.[3]

According to scientists, the age of the gujots corresponds with the end of the last glaciation, i.e. 11000 — 12000 years ago. It's hard not to notice that it matches the age of the "3 peoples — 1 language empire," as ascertained by Professor Szalek, the time when the "ways of migrations" began to differentiate. Some geologists even believe that the process of sinking continued in historic times. In one of Kondratov's books he recounts an opinion of such a scientist, who wrote that: "We may risk a claim that quite recently, perhaps partially under our very eyes, the Pacific Ocean has expanded significantly at the expense of the adjacent continents…" [3]

It's a particularly significant fact that a whole chain of such gujots crowns the underwater "Nazca ridge" that runs almost straight from Easter Island to the South American coast, or more exactly, to the area where the most interesting cultures mushroomed later on. The gujots there have tops at the depth of 200-500 meters, although the ridge itself lies at the depth of 1-2 kilometers. It generally matches the stories of the sinking lands quite perfectly. In the aforementioned book on the Hopi myths by J. Blumrich, the Hopi chief described the migration as "jumping from one island to another, while they successively sank under the waves"; he said this clearly in reference to the oceanic migration from the South Pacific to South America. If we assume that the "Nazca gujots" were present there before the end of the last ice age, then we must come to the conclusion that at that time there was hardly any major "oceanic gap" dividing Easter Island from the continent at all. Certainly it was a lot more convenient route than the thousands-mile long Arctic one.

And if we go this far, it's worth considering what the facts related with the coming of Indians to America may contribute to the "Pacific axis" riddle. As I have mentioned, it is one of the "keys."

(Footnotes)

* That is, some 6.6 pounds.

** Or just over two feet.

*** *Kaskara and the Seven Worlds*

An old print of a long eared Inca.

Left: A golden figure of an Inca, with elongated ears, found in Chile. Bottom: Petroglyphs from Pedra Furada, Chile (Drawing by I. Witkowski).

Top: The trilithon on Tongatapu drawn by James Churchward in 1876. Middle: The
Tonga pyramids in an old print. Bottom: One of the largest stones on Tonga.

95

Writing given to John Macmillan Brown from Olei Island in Micronesia showing a now extinct written language.

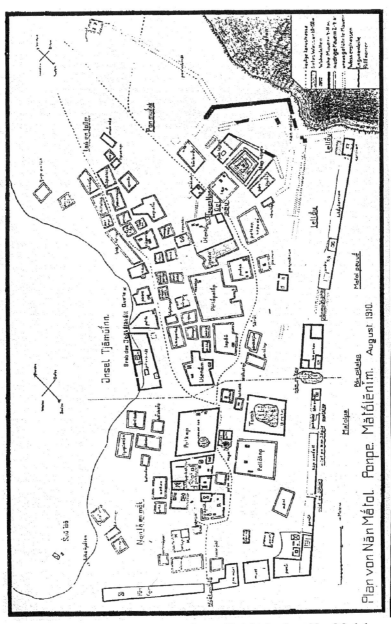

Hambruch's 1910 map of the extensive artificial islands at Nan Madol.

An old photo of the gigantic walls on Kosrae Island.

4

THE MYSTERIOUS ORIGIN OF THE AMERICAN INDIANS

One has to ask oneself a fundamental question: if the Protodravidians reached as far as Easter Island, then why wouldn't they go a couple of thousands miles further? After all—this tiny piece of rock doesn't seem to be a valuable "objective" of any pre-planned migration.

As we know from textbooks, there is officially no mystery. But these textbooks don't incorporate many of the findings, especially the new ones. Before we pass to them, however, it's good to look at the generally accepted theory pertaining to the origin(s) of the American Indians.

Formulated in 1938, it was accepted by the scientific community. Its author was a renowned employee of the Museum of Natural History in New York, as well as the Smithsonian Institution. Dr. Alex Hrdlicka was born in what later became Czechoslovakia, but he was in fact Austro-Hungarian. He declared that all American natives arrived from Asia via the so-called Beringia, the bridge of land between eastern Siberia and Alaska, that emerged from Bering Sea after the water accumulated in the form of glaciers.

They are supposed to be basically the same people who still inhabit the lands in question, such as the Inuits living in Canada, hordes of hunter-gatherers who have ventured far north, perhaps chasing or tracking migrating prey. Of course, after crossing the glacier covering the entirety of today's Canada and a large part of the US, they supposedly moved further south, in due measure taking new territories under their control. At the end of the last glaciation they reached the Rockies, then the Great Plains, and so on. According to Hrdlicka it was a continuous trek southward, via Central America to the Andes and the Amazon basin, then down to the Land of Fire (Tierra del Fuego), the southernmost tip of the South American continent.

Hrdlicka claimed initially that it could not have begun earlier than some five thousand years ago. Why such a figure? I'm not sure if he himself would be able to provide a specific answer to that question. It is based officially on stratigraphy, the chronology of the deposits in which certain man-made artifacts were found, but there was no way then to date such layers in an objective way, to provide specific dates. However, shortly after World War Two, Hrdlicka shifted that timeline to around 12,000 years before the present, which coincided with the end of the Ice Age. Only in the 1950s did the first objective method of dating appear on the archaeological scene: radiocarbon dating. Eventually a more or less comprehensive chronology of migrations started to be constructed by scientists. The theory started to become more and more questionable (although some aspects have survived the successive waves of scrutiny). But even before such tools became available, one could point out specific weak points of the now regnant theory of Hrdlicka.

First of all it implies that all the migrants represented a single anthropological type. In other words they would all have to be Mongoloids, the same, and the *only* kind of people that have left traces and remains along the supposed track in the Arctic (i.e., not only in Alaska or the Rockies, but also in eastern Siberia). That seemed naive for many scholars even then, for there is great anthropological variety among Indians (or American Indians, "Amerindians"), especially in South America. The theory of evolution was of course well known even in the 1930s and it was obvious that such diversification could not be a product of evolution in the time scale that Hrdlicka adhered to so desperately. If the people diversified, adapting to their new environments through a process of evolution, it would have taken a very long time. But a much earlier use of the northern route would make the migration more difficult, if not impossible, due to the unavailability of ground not covered by ice. Moreover, the evidence which was unearthed later, proving that people were present in America earlier, effectively undermined the whole theory. And then there were the anthropologists, or even geographers, dealing with South America (mostly South Americans), who saw these chronological contradictions very clearly, but such notions rarely penetrated the barrier of the North American "academic circle."

At any rate, the most obvious evidence against such a theory has been conveniently omitted, without any credible explanation. More or less at the same time, anthropology experienced a very interesting period of studying "cultural traces," mostly by ethnographers, which led to the gathering of a mountain of materials proving that the issue of origins, in the case of the oldest cultures and civilizations, is much more complex than Hrdlicka assumed at that time. Some outstanding scholars devoted their lives to this idea, such as Robert Heine-Geldern, Erland Nordenskjöld, Dick Edgar Ibarra–Grasso, and later the brilliant amateur Thor Heyerdahl. They were mostly Europeans or South Americans, such as Ibarra–Grasso; North American science was absent and still isn't very much interested in this research—eventually it was effectively forgotten, despite being the key to understanding the first civilizations.

Another fundamental implication of Hrdlicka's theory that was in practicality unjustified, was that there should be visible a clear chronological chain of development along the "north–south axis." Cultural remains from North America should be clearly older than those from Central America, and those in turn should be significantly older than the South American ones. In other words, the youngest cultures should be from the far south, or at any rate there shouldn't be anything very *old* in the far south. That too was quite bizarre as a scientific idea, for there is no such clear correlation. For example: if we take a look at a map of Central America showing the chronology of cultures, the following order will emerge. Let's start from the southern section of Central America:

1. We will see the Olmecs, which was the oldest civilization there. The first remains date from the 12th century B.C., the last ones from the first century B.C. They occupied the territory of the southernmost part of Mexico and Guatemala.
2. In the adjacent territory, slightly to the west, emerged, in the 5th century B.C., a similar culture of Zapotecs and Mixtecs. It lasted quite a long time and disappeared from

101

the scene in the 15th century A.D.

3. At the same latitude, or more precisely, in the territory occupied earlier by the Olmecs, flourished the Mayan civilization, for around 1000 years, beginning in the 1st century B.C. And then the great trek northward began.

4. In the 2nd century A.D. there appeared the Teotihuacan civilization in central Mexico. It was succeeded by the Toltecs and the Aztecs, who were the youngest, and at the same time, the most northern Central American civilization.

5. The only cultural center in today's US that possessed a city—the Casas Grande—appeared only in the 7th century A.D., almost two thousand years *after* the Olmecs in the south.

How is this supposed to support the migration from the north? Such a route was used, there's no doubt about it, but it might not be the oldest or the most important one. The picture isn't that simple.

South American scholars were probably the first who saw the contradictions and weaknesses in Hrdlicka's theory. Emilio Romero, a Peruvian professor of San Marcos University in Lima and the chairman of the Peruvian Geographic Society, wrote the following in his book entitled *Biografia de los Andes (Biography of the Andes)*, which was published in 1965 in Peru. In the following citation the emphasis is by me:

> All these undertakings of primitive man were taken probably in small groups or pairs, which, moving step by step forward, accommodated themselves to the new conditions, which were the altitude, drought and climatic changes. Prehistoric man's foray to move out of the realm of the tropics, the somberness of the steppes or coastal deserts, lasted probably for many centuries, and we will never learn anything about what was going on at these times. *But the man who conquered the Andes was undoubtedly a fully modern type, with a completely*

revolutionary store of experiences and ideas when compared to the primitive peoples' mentality.

This new migratory wave probably arrived from somewhere in the south, for there exists an unblurred path that marks the track of the new cultures from the Argentine foothills of the Andes and the Atacama desert up to the great centers of Tiahuanaco (Bolivia), which ran along Lake Titicaca's shore leading to Cuzco—the top achievement of the prehispanic civilizations in South America.

If these were groups coming from Asian oceanic islands, which used their navigating experience and the presence of numerous islands —which later disappeared, but geologists admit that they might have existed—then one can presume that the incomers from Polynesia *brought with themselves* conceptions differing from the notions of the primitive inhabitants akin to the Mongols from central Asia, that came through the Bering Strait.

Unfortunately, North American archaeology treats the peopling of the continent in complete isolation from the migrations in the Pacific basin.

As has been shown on a respective map in time, in South America, were discovered remains that were not only older than North American human remains, but even older than those in the entirety of eastern Siberia. Still, there are no certain traces of people from North America (USA and Canada) that would be older than approximately 15,000 years. From South America there is, in turn, a steady influx of datings that are undermining the generally accepted theory.

One of the most publicized discoveries has taken place in southeastern Brazil, i.e., very far from the Bering bridge. The inhabitants had to cross, among other things, the vastness of the great Amazon jungle first. The place is named Pedra Furada and in the 1980s it was to become the archaeological sensation of the century. In an inhospitable mountain region, in the outskirts of the

Mato Grosso jungle, there are a lot of natural hideouts—recesses in exposed rock faces or overhangs, places that archaeologists call "rockshelters." They were ideal to house human settlements, or temporary camps. Because there is a steady supply of sediments covering the successive layers with dirt, and dust falling or being washed over from above, these are ideal excavation sites, for they tended to be used by various groups of settlers, in various epochs. Under one such overhang, a group of scientists found, as early as 1963, a series of interesting petroglyphs (or drawings on the faces of rocks). Soon after that excavations began, naturally, in order to ascertain the time when their creators stayed in this place. As usual, the deeper the researchers dug, the older were the remains—and they were quite old indeed! The press from all over the world—and not just the professional journals—chronicled the excavations' progress, and quoted older and older dates. Eventually, after many years, the scientists reached the oldest sediments of charcoal, leftovers from the innumerable campfires that must have been used through the millennia. The age of the remains of tools and other artifacts from this deepest layer was quite unbelievable: they were almost *50,000 years old!* It meant turning the entire American prehistory upside down, and of course, it also meant the revision of the existing theories. The French popular scientific magazine *Science et Vie* presented, in 1988, the following description of Pedra Furada:

> But the remote past emerges by itself, without participation of the scientists, thanks to these petroglyphs. They bear testimony to the very high level of the civilization that created them, comparable with the one known from the prehistory of Europe. The correlation is shocking.
>
> The age of the oldest traces of such drawings found in the caves of southern France is estimated to be 32 thousand years. But these are, as has been said, traces without substantial meaning. The 30 thousand year old drawings portray figures, or their fragments, allowing us to guess about the whole. It seems that man has mastered artistic techniques

104

some 17 thousand years ago and the peak period
in the development of European prehistoric art is
dated for the time of 15—10 thousand years ago.
This art vanishes gradually along with the decline of
the hunting period and the advent of agriculture.

Only a few years ago the researchers of
prehistory didn't even suppose that the New
Continent may be hiding treasures of cave art as
old as the European specimen. And here it turns
out that there are thousands of petroglyphs! And
perhaps other ones are waiting for their turn in the
inaccessible and poorly populated regions?

Some archaeologists later questioned the value of the
discoveries from Pedra Furada, claiming that they weren't that
sure that the deepest charcoal layers indeed contained remains of
man-made artifacts. Nevertheless, the problem of chronology in
the peopling of the American continents has not disappeared at all,
because it wasn't the only such place that undermined the reigning
academic theories.

As Professor Machowski, a Polish scholar specializing in
oceanic migrations, has written:

Soon a woman appeared on the scientific horizon,
who has forced the scholars to shift the dates back,
into much earlier times. She was "Minnesota
Minnie," as she was playfully nicknamed by some
student. In fact, it was a skeleton of a 15-year old
girl, unearthed in 1932 from a depth of 4 meters,
by workers constructing a road in Minnesota.
On the basis of her skull's and teeth's features it
was ascertained that she was a Mongoloid with a
admixture of the early white race. The Minnesota
Man's age—for this is "her" official name—was
determined by the anthropologist Dr. .A. E. Jenks
as twenty thousand years!...

In the coming years, as a result of toilsome
searches, many more traces of the human presence

in America were found, some as old as 25,000 years. The most sensational discovery, which amazed the scientific community, was made almost fifty years ago.

In 1956, a certain archaeologist came across, in the town of Lewisville, Texas, some traces of human occupation that appear in the archaeological annals under the codename "the Lewisville Man." His remains were subjected to laboratory examination with the help of the C14 method, only five years old at that time, but already generally accepted as reliable and relatively precise. The outcome turned out to be so sensational, that many scientists simply didn't want to believe them. The examined samples were 37,000 years old. At that time it was the oldest and irrefutably confirmed evidence for the early human presence on the American continent. [41]

Strangely enough, this discovery was soon forgotten by archaeologists, probably because of the very fact that it shattered the theory; it was just too "weird!"

A familiar thread, again emerging from this description, is the aforementioned "admixture," suggesting a route other than the northern route, an alternative path of migration, and therefore implying an alternative origin of certain civilizations. Professor Machowski described yet another interesting episode in the research: [41]

Dr A. Wiercinski, during his stay in Mexico, has examined ...human skulls originating from pre-Columbian times, among others the "Tepexan man"—one of the oldest human remains discovered on the American continent, dated as 10-12 thousand years old, as well as approximately one hundred Neolithic skulls from Tlatilco. In total this anthropologist has examined and photographed over 320 skulls belonging to various groups of people, which created the old centers of civilizations—

Olmecs, Mayas, Mixtecs and Zapotecs...

The results of his research have confirmed the existence of the traces of white, as well as black, races in Central America. Both part of the skulls, as well as realistic depictions of human figures, exhibit the features characteristic for the representatives of the so-called Armenoidal race, the original settlements of which were located in Asia Minor.*

As a result of great prehistoric migrations this population has spread out in Europe, reaching as far as today's Spain.**

The hardest nut to crack, in changing the prehistoric picture of America was yet to come, from South America once again, more precisely from the border area between central and southern Chile in the extreme south—in other words, where people were not supposed to be very early.

This place is known as Monte Verde and it lies at the latitude of 41.5°S, in a cool climatic zone exposed to Antarctic winds and sea currents, 950 km (590 miles) south from the country's capital, Santiago, or 1500 km (930 miles) north from the southernmost tip of the continent. What has been uncovered there is the earliest known prehistoric permanent settlement, used for as long as thousands of years. This means simply a permanent village, which in turn implies that the inhabitants had a relatively developed agriculture, and therefore probably were not hunter-gatherers, contrary to the case of almost the entirety of such peoples in North America.

The ruins of around a dozen wooden buildings or huts have been cleared out, characterized by a kind of grid system. Apparently the roofs sheltered not only the buildings, but also the streets or sidewalks, which shouldn't amaze us if we take into account that it's a wet region, with high precipitation; around 150 days with rainfall or snowfall per year, on average. It's just an area with a strong maritime climatic influence, and apparently it was so in distant times too. Fragments of wooden tools, as well as potatoes, were found which substantiated the earlier suspicion that it was a strictly rural, agricultural community.

The fact that there was a village in such a remote place—far

107

from the "mythical" Bering bridge—wouldn't be so amazing if not for the fact that the first dating, from a relatively shallow layer, provided dates as distant as 12,000–13,000 years! The amazement on the part of North American scientists, commanded by Tom Dillehay, who became famous after this, was all the greater in that they realized that they saw here the ruins of probably the oldest permanent human settlement of such a kind in *both* Americas.

Soon after that, Dillehay somewhat shyly announced that man-made artifacts have been extracted from a layer that was 33,000 years old. It met with disbelief on the part of most of the community, although even in a "cautious" book (but a very good one) describing the peopling of Americas, such information has been presented, albeit only as a caption under a photograph— "Biface from the earliest occupation at Monte Verde. This specimen may date to 33.000 B.P." [42]—without any further comment!

Can you believe it? Organized society in such a remote corner in the 310th century B.C. It would be the *oldest* agricultural society on our planet, around five times older (!) than the oldest agricultural society known so far, from the Middle East. Something is again wrong with this picture, especially if we take into account the fact that the North American Indians never developed beyond the Stone Age, despite probably much better conditions to develop efficient agriculture. I quote a very characteristic description from the aforementioned book on the peopling of America, this time referring to Monte Verde, with emphasis by me, as usual:

> The Monte Verdeans were probably a group of incipient colonizers in the region, moving in at a time when the glaciers were rapidly receding and the immediate area of the Maullin River was a cool, temperate wetland forest circled by a variety of other habitats and ecological zones. And there they pursued a lifeway *far more sophisticated* and sedentary than what anybody had expected for such early inhabitants of the hemisphere.
>
> To many who read about this, it just did not seem right. The dates were *alarming*, of course. It meant that people had been living in what appears

to be something like a village, something certainly more socially complex than a band of wandering hunters and gatherers, 10,000 miles south of the Bering land bridge, more than a thousand years before Clovis Man[***] had reached Arizona....

But aside from the awkward—actually impossible—dates at Monte Verde, the artifacts were all wrong. Some bifaces, a lot of primitive unifaces, and all that other junk. More than one commentator asked: "what planet did these people come from?" The question reflected awe in some and skepticism in others. The Monte Verdeans simply did not meet the expectations of those who were locked into a Clovis-inspired theory of the peopling of the hemisphere. (Remember the role of expectations in this entire story, starting with the unlikelihood that the Indians could have piled up dirt into grand mounds).[42]

Scientific American magazine wrote that, "The relatively high level of social development represented by the Monte Verde community indicates that the cultures of the New World in the upper Pleistocene were far more complex than was previously thought."

Of course, this once again forced scientists to reconsider the Bering bridge theory and to rethink the question of American civilizations' origins in general, a question with potentially powerful implications. Once again, I will return to the book cited above, written by one of the most distinguished American archaeologists:

Serious questions remain about Topper, Saltville and Cactus Hill, and these sites will indeed benefit from continuing investigation and confirmation. Yet with such sites coming to the fore and Meadowcroft and Monte Verde already securely established as pre-Clovis, except in the minds of fanatics, the days of Clovis First are finally over and the old questions can arise, fresh and wonderful to behold. Who are those guys? How did they get here? When? Scenarios for pre-Clovis migration abound, ranging from the conservative to the freebooting. Brian Fagan, an indefatigable chronicler of American archaeology in both textbooks and popular books, as well as a professor of anthropology at the University of California at Santa Barbara and an early and vocal supporter of Meadowcroft, expresses a cautious view in his latest college-level textbook on world prehistory. He assumes that most human activity on the continent dates from sometime after 20,000 years ago and that practically no one lived in Siberia before 18,000 years ago, neither of which are unreasonable suggestions based on a conservative interpretation of available data. Similarly, few people lived in frigid Beringia during the glacial maximum, but then, about 12,700 B.C. or 14,650 years ago the temperatures in the far north rose rapidly and people began heading across the land bridge and south. Once under way, they ranged far and wide.

Computer modeling, Fagan says, suggests that if people took the "least-cost" approach to all this pioneering—meaning that they took the least arduous routes into the unknown places that would provide them with food and good stone for tools— they would have needed only two millenia to settle the New World from polar bear land to penguinville. But this is a linear approach, and the sites of early human habitation do not necessarily obey linear rules. Indeed, they do not appear to be linear at all but rather are scaterred thinly over huge regions, which suggests that people leapfrogged their way into the New World, settling some areas and ignoring others. Then, he suggests, Clovis people came along and filled in the blanks on the map.

110

For by 11,400 years ago, North America entered into the Younger Dryas, the cold snap mentioned earlier, which could have caused wetter and more favorable game conditions on the Great Plains and in the Southwest and allowed Clovis folk to flourish, spread out, and adapt to a wide range of environments, its artifacts diversifying by what he calls "stylistic drift."

As Fagan says, this picture is "still little more than a theoretical scenario," and indeed it leaves many questions unanswered....

Perhaps the biggest problem I have with Fagan's otherwise quite plausible scenario is that he still has the initial percolation of humans into the New World pegged at about 14,000 B.P., which gives them only about 1500 years to reach Monte Verde [!?—I.W.] and another 1300 years to populate the rest of the hemisphere. Despite the fact that this is a much longer time than Martin or Haynes allows for the penetration of the hemisphere, it is still, at least in my mind, too short to provide enough time to adjust and adapt to the 8000 miles of mountains, rain forests, plains and deserts with their ever-changing array of potential game and plant food resources. Remember, each new habitat offers not only potentially novel plant and animal foods, but also new medicinal and/or poisonous plants at each step. One false bite and you're dead or hallucinating for a week. More seriously, Fagan's alloted colonization interval seems too short to account for the great diversity in technology and lifestyles that seem to be well established by 11,000 years ago, and further, his numbers seem too brief in comparison to the documented colonization rates for either interior Australia or Northern Europe during deglaciation....

As we have seen ..., that process simply had to take a lot more than a few centuries or even a few millenia. The rapidity with which we today adopt whole new technologies can confuse us about the deep past and make us forget how slowly traditional human societies change....

The big problem presented by the existence of pre-Clovis sites is that, for all anyone can tell, the ice-free corridor between the Cordilleran and Laurentian glaciers was open around early Clovis time, but *it had been shut for several thousand years before that. The only likely solution is that they must have come by boat....*

That may be getting pretty speculative, but it is a fact that people got to Australia at least 40,000 years ago, and they could have gotten there only by some sort of watercraft over open water. Why would such a maritime folk decide to go only south?...

Today, the study of the early peopling of the New World is vibrant and alive with possibilities. The questions with which we began this book and this chapter—who were those guys, when did they get here, and how?—remain without definitive answers. What we can say is that we have peeled back a lot of layers of ignorance over the past century or so. At the very least, we now know better who these guys weren't: they were neither the lost tribes of Israel nor the Atlanteans, they weren't Neanderthal-like, and they didn't get here only a few thousand years ago. They weren't a single band of anyone, much less a band of fifty or a hundred turbocharged hunters.

Today there are multiple routes to explore, multiple times to pin down, multiple groups of people who were potentially those early pioneers. Whereas a hundred years ago the archaeologist's quiver had very few arrows, today an expanding host of new disciplines and subdisciplines is brought to bear on the old questions, each in turn raising new questions to the new answers, which then raise even more questions. [42]

We will return again to the oldest civilizations of South America, for most of this book is in fact an introduction letting us understand their greatest achievement (that being Puma Punku, described at the end of the present work). But what should be borne in mind is that it was this continent that became the scene of the most interesting, even breathtaking achievements—the continent that supposedly was peopled at the very last. It's a necessary introduction, for without it the unraveling of the challenging mystery, would not be possible. It illustrates how strange and intriguing it really is: as different from the present archaeological dogmas (although based on facts) as the sophisticated blocks from Puma Punku are different from anything else from the first centuries A.D.—and not just from South America!

Let me insert here a short remark in order to avoid misunderstandings: this book is not about "where did the Indians (Amerindians) in general come from?" but about "where did the creators of one, forgotten (and truly *outstanding*, strange) civilization come from?" It was a specific people, *as "strange," as the blocks themselves.*

Such a "quantum leap" in civilization, which Monte Verde alone illustrates, can be explained generally in two ways: (1) either they came with an already developed cultural storehouse of knowledge that generated the development; or, (2) unknown factors came into play that have in some unclear way artificially accelerated their developmental path. The latter may seem far-out, but *it will really become evident* when we come to the last chapter. To speak frankly, the first possibility doesn't rule out the other. Moving the cradle of this forgotten culture to another continent or some lost land doesn't in fact solve anything. It only creates another question: what was the real source of these achievements; where, and what, was the real mechanism behind the origin of these roots? It's simply hard to comprehend, while staying within the conventional understanding of these things, how in one place in the world cultures could experience such an "impossible" boost, by thousands or perhaps even tens of thousands of years, while in other parts of the world no such a processes were visible. It's of course the re-emergence of the same problem that was raised by the "Axis of the World" (Mohenjo Daro—Nan Madol—Easter Island): what sort of process could give them such a geographic knowledge of the world that enabled the establishment of three specific centers in such geometrically cardinal points on the surface of our planet? And what were they for? Who was supposed to "read" this message?

I repeat this dilemma because it's still relevant in the South American context as well as in the case of the "Axis" itself. It's all just a fragment of one continuous chain of "impossible facts"— and they all form one consistent whole when we look at them from a right perspective.

So, lets deal with the next link.

In the local museum in the Argentine town of San Juan—in the far south again!—there exists, in very good condition the oldest human mummy in the world. It is around 9000 years old and has been excavated from the Los Morillos graveyard in the foothills of the nearby Andes. The oldest known Egyptian mummy is around 5000 years old—hence it's almost two times younger! We used to think of ancient Egypt as almost a synonym of antiquity, didn't we?

Perhaps it's a remarkable fact, and not merely a coincidence, that at the Pacific coast of neighboring Chile—just on the other side of the Andes, and at almost the same latitude as Easter Island—there is quite an abundance of mummies, almost as old as the one from San Juan. They are known as the Chinchorro mummies. Because they were found on the desert coast of the Atacama desert, the driest place on Earth, it's a widely accepted fact that the people that later became the mummies were fishermen and probably sailors in general; there are, and were, just no other sources of food. The implications of this fact don't penetrate, obviously, the vast majority of scientific minds—yet. It's hard to avoid the reflection, in light of the mummies and Monte Verde, that it is Chile that emerges as the place where *the oldest* remains of organized, sedentary societies are being found. The oldest on our planet!

And it's not the only such place. The entire central and

southern Pacific coast of South America is a "land of mummies." I know this to be a fact, for I saw examples when I was in Peru in 1997. I went then to visit an old cemetery, right in the middle of the desert, some 80 km 9or 50 miles) south of Nazca, the famous location where the giant geoglyphs on the plateau can be seen, but only from a plane! The place is called Chauchilla and is hardly known to outsiders. After a long ride along the bumpy, stony road I finally spotted something that looked suspicious at first glance. The landscape was generally flat, yellowish-grey, just a stony desert. Somewhere in the distance there was, however, a group of mounds, covering a rather large area. When I approached I noticed that the yellowish desert floor around was specked with some snow-white objects. These were bones bleached by the ultraviolet rays of the Sun, scattered all over the place. The cemetery was robbed continuously for decades and that's what generally was left; only very few graves survived that almost industrial exploitation. I looked around and I spotted something other than white, something black and elongated. I went closer and took a better look. It was a braid. I grasped it; it was long, black and still very soft, as if cut off yesterday. At the end there hung a part of the head, part of the skull with the rest of the hair. There was no shortage of pottery at the site, but all broken in pieces. These were the objects that were considered useless by the robbers. They were interested only in one thing; you canguess what.

There is simply such an abundance of cemeteries, ruins and so on there, that it is just impossible to guard them all—that's a relatively new concept, yet in the 1950s Peru was an Eldorado, waiting to be explored in this respect. The problem is, of course, that the robbers destroyed the vast majority of their findings, without even a shadow of bad conscience. So, if we consider that the Spanish conquistadors carried out a planned policy of wiping the ancient heritage out, then it will become clear that what is left is just a tiny fraction of the original picture, of the truth. The Spaniards, among other things, almost completely exterminated the ancient aristocracy, assuming that only they constituted a real threat to their economy based on the re-introduction of slavery (the infamous *encomiendas*, where the colonizers were granted specific lands along with the natives living there, as a property). This policy

115

of a planned destruction of the existing social structures meant, however, an irreversible loss for history, because in the ancient societies it was only the narrow ruling layer that possessed the knowledge about their past. For example, agriculture experienced a period of deterioration, because no one knew how to maintain the ancient system of irrigation channels and terraces (water also preserved the crops from freezing in the higher mountains). As a result, the efficiency of local agriculture, which probably had no equivalent in the ancient world, dropped by an order of magnitude. This pertains mostly to the "Andean" countries: to today's Peru, Ecuador and Bolivia.

Let me return, however, for a moment to the issue of sedentary societies in South America, which is quite important because it is clear evidence for an "accelerated" path of development there. Monte Verde is not the only place where agriculture appeared suspiciously early and permanent settlements were built.

In another place on the Peruvian coast, known as the Guitarrero cave near the country's capital, scientists have discovered evidence for the cultivation of beans and pepper in sediments from the ninth millennium B.C.[18]

Another such example can be found on the Pacific coast of Ecuador, almost on the equator, as the country's name itself suggests. The distinction between the "Old" and "New" worlds is therefore purely symbolic — the Andean cultures not only matched the ones from the Middle East, thought so far to be the oldest — but in some respects may boast even deeper-reaching roots. As far as the Middle East is concerned, it is commonly thought that *the first* evidence of agriculture — the cultivation of crops — appeared there around 7000 years B.C., or 9000 years ago. However, strange as it may seem, it had *already* appeared in South America in many places on the western coast by that time.

In southern Ecuador, among other places on St. Helen Island, American archaeologists uncovered the remains of a strange culture which was named Las Vegas, after one of the nearby towns. The evidence unearthed delivered compelling evidence that the inhabitants cultivated a number of crops, including maize, as early as 8500 years ago; that is, they had developed agriculture at the time when their Middle Eastern counterparts were still at a very initial stage. And again, on the path running across the Pacific, we are finding facts completely shattering our knowledge about the beginnings of human culture.

Why, however, is Ecuadorian culture said to be "strange"? It's not just about the timing!

The thread started with a discovery made by a local amateur, Emilio Estrada, as far back as 1956. He found suspicously thick deposits of sea shells on the Ecuadorian coast. Soon after starting to excavate them, in the Guayas province, he also found a lot of ancient pottery—or rather fragments of it. Estrada died in 1961, soon after he realized that the pottery didn't resemble anything known from other parts of this continent, but his work was continued by North American archaeologists, intrigued by what he had noticed.[41]

The oldest Ecuadorian cultures were eventually subjected to very careful research by scientists from the American Smithsonian Institution, mostly in the 1980s. Their results have forced them to completely revise the existing schemes. It turned out, for example, that the pottery left after the Valdivia culture, which existed in Ecuador from the fourth millennium B.C., was very characteristic. It was virtually identical to the oldest Japanese pottery, created by the first inhabitants of the Japanese islands, the Jomon people, who were mentioned earlier. The fact that it apparently appeared in South America quite suddenly was also strange. The team that carried out excavations near Valdivia even undertook an expedition to Japan, to the archaeological sites and towns of Ataka and Sobata on Kiusiu Island, in order to compare their findings with the Japanese equivalents.

The Jomon are classified by the anthropologists as members of the so-called Ainuidal peoples, *which actually means that they were the Japanese descendants of the same "branch" of the white people which left their mummies in the Chinese Tarim Basin,* who continued their migration eastwards to Japan, and up to South America, as the Smithsonian Institute's research proved: the Ainu, especially from Honsiu Island, had white skin. By the way: it was the same culture that left the "dogu" figures, portraying men in "spacesuits," with helmets equipped with "vizors" on their heads. The scientists from the Smithsonian Institute have also proven that the Valdivia culture was, among others, the first one in the world which mastered smelting of platinum—a metal that melts in a very high temperature—1770 °C (over 3200 °F). Strangely enough, platinum also appears in reference to Nan Madol, but we will return to that later. Generally, it's compelling evidence confirming that the bearers of civilization did not come from the north, from Alaska at all. It wasn't however the only trace of the Ainuidal migration(s) to America—we will return to that.

The Valdivia (Ecuador) and Jomon (Japan) pottery was identical in every respect; all the ornaments and decorations were virtually the same! This also proves, beyond a shadow of a doubt, *that seafarers have brought this cultural heritage with them to South America*—straight from another continent! This thread prompted me to reach for Graham Hancock's book entitled *Underworld*, which actually deals quite extensively (740 pages) with the oldest Japanese cultures, including the Ainuidal. Once again I found there a piece of history as if from another planet, and as I mentioned, it's *one link in a chain of traces*:

> As recently as 1998 most scholars believed that the oldest Jomon pottery was made about 12,500 years ago—itself a *staggeringly early date*—but so rapid is the pace of new discovery in this field, that the origins of Jomon civilization have had to be continuously revised backwards.
>
> In May 2000, on my second visit to the Aomori area, I held in the palm of my hand four fragments of a broken Jomon pot 16,500 years old. Excavated at a site known as Odayamamaoto No. 1 Iseki, the potsherds had been dated using state-of-the-art AMS technology.
>
> It is still a little known fact that the Jomon of Japan are the world's oldest pottery-making culture. But even less well known is the extent to which this prehistoric people maintained a distinct identity as a single, homogenous group. According to Dr Yasuhiro Okada, the Aomori Prefecture's Chief Archaeologist at Sannai-Muruyama, "they

were one culture, from beginning to the end."

Imagine that—one culture, probably one language, probably one religion, staying intact for more than 14,000 years….

Then in April 2000 I visited Uenohara, a much older Jomon site on the island of Kyushu. Kuzanori Aozaki, one of the prefecture's archaeologists, explained that Uenohara had been a continuously inhabited settlement over a 2000-year period from roughly 9500 to 7500 years ago. "They had their lives pretty well worked out; he explained; at any one time they had more than 100 people living here. They were comfortable… I would even say prosperous. All their basic needs were met. They had ample food, good shelter, comfortable, elegant clothing."

—"And this was a permanent settlement, like a village or a small town?"

—"Yes."

—"But doesn't that contradict the idea of the Jomon as simple hunter-gatherers?"

—"Yes, it does…

Another intriguing recent discovery is that as far back as 8000 years ago the Jomon were cultivating a non-indigenous plant, the bottle-gourd, which palaeo-biological studies indicate must have been imported from Africa. There is also some evidence of the cultivation of beans at a very early date. Indeed, according to profesor Tatsuo Kobayashi, the Jomon made effective use of nearly every species of available plants and animals—"a conscious and rational use of nature's bounty with a low level use of less desired species to avoid depletion of preferred ones."…

But it was Sahara Makoto, the Director-General of the National Museum of Japanese History, who dropped the biggest bombshell on my preconceptions about the Jomon. When I met him

119

on 17 May 2000 he told me quite casually of new evidence that had just come his way, unconfirmed as yet but startling if true, which suggested that the Jomon could have been cultivating rice as early as 12,000 years ago…

Now suddenly here was the dizzying possibility that the Jomon could have been growing rice *deep in the Old Stone Age,* thousands of years before anybody else…

—"If that's true it's a revolution, isn't it?" I stuttered. [43]

Despite the groundbreaking discoveries made by the Smithsonian Institution, the Valdivia culture is even less well known.

In part, this stems from the fact that it isn't particularly developed and not even in a very hospitable part of the world. I had the opportunity of checking it out, on my own, during a visit in 1997. Actually I was in Colombia, but I decided to turn aside from the prearranged route in order to gather some materials on this "forgotten" place, and its history, of course. The "optimal plan" was to get to the actual archaeological sites on the coast and perhaps to chat with some scholars; the "minimal variant" was to visit the local museum and take some snapshots of the exhibits.

This episode, although brief, turned out to be one of the most shocking in my career as a journalist and researcher. I will allow myself to describe it at length, although it doesn't contribute very much to the main issue: the origin of the local civilizations. Hence I have separated this section with asterisks.

*   *   *

My adventure began in October of 1997 in Bogota, the capital of Colombia. There I boarded an Ecuadorian plane of their national carrier, SAETA. It was supposed to fly to the city of Guayaquil on the coast, with a stopover in the capital, Quito. It was in fact my first encounter with this country, and the first shock.

The fact that it was a Boeing 727 in a model not manufactured for about 30 years was nothing. I haven't seen such a plane ever in my life and there is a quite a good chance that I will never see anything similar again! Along with the other passengers, I approached the plane's door walking on the so-called taxiway. This provided the first sensations of foreboding. It was hard not to spot the holes in the aluminum plating of the wing, patched with an epoxy-resin, apparently of the kind used for cars. What was most amazing, however, was that it was applied rather clumsily, probably just with a finger. Apparently nobody was bothered about keeping the aerodynamic profile. I never imagined, in my bravest nightmares, that something like that was possible at all.

But, well—I won't run away. I walk on.

Entering the cabin was another shock—as could be expected. Over 50% of North Americans fly regularly, so probably everyone knows what a plane looks like inside, or *should* look like. Seats, floor, windows, ceiling in the form of plastic panels—all that taken for granted. Here, however, it wasn't the case. The ceiling panels, for example, were in pieces. The fragments hung over the passing passengers, decorated with shreds of something that looked like white glass-wool, hanging fancifully and rubbing against the passengers' heads. Above that were exposed, twisted aluminum pipes of various diameters, and cables, etc. I sat in the last row, because the last rows were empty, and to increase the chances of survival. As it has soon turned out, they were to be used by the crew, but there were a lot of empty seats, so they left me in peace. Thanks to this, I was the only passenger who was able to observe the reactions of the cabin crew during the flight.

I sat and pulled the seat's arm down, wanting to rotate it to a horizontal position. It fell on the floor, without attracting anybody's attention. I've grasped the safety belt. It was left in my hands. I could have rolled it and put it into my pocket. I still regret that I didn't taken a souvenir of the journey.

Miraculously this unbelievable pile of scrap took off and, quite strangely, it was flying. I was seized with some weird apathy, a state of helplessness. I started staring at one of the holes in a panel above, unbelievably encrusted with dirt. In my head appeared a surreal vision of a row of cockroaches coming out of it, one after another. Indeed, several of them left this hideout after a while!

After a modest meal the scrap started to dodge between the mountains, approaching Ecuador's capital, Quito. At some moment I started having the impression however, that it was not just dodging. On the basis of my aerospace knowledge and experience, I came to the irrefutable conviction that the old 727 had a serious problem with the control system, specifically with vertical control. Momentarily it descended abruptly, then suddenly popped up. The movements seemed to be completely uncoordinated. I wasn't sure that was really the case, but the cabin crew, sitting just in front of me, on the other side of the aisle, very effectively dispelled any doubts. At the moments of sudden descents they froze, as in a freeze-frame. The staff pulled out those small bottles of alcohol (not for passengers, apparently) and emptied one after another in rapid succession, straight from the bottle. Not for a moment were they aware of my existence, not a single glance. They just paid no attention to anything else.

I have to admit that it was one of very few moments in my life when I resigned myself to death. I wasn't thinking about what might come later.

Well, it wasn't "that" moment yet, for we eventually reached our destination.

I left the airport in haste, reached a taxicab waiting in front of the building and blindly decided to look for some hotel—it was middle of the night. I could therefore take a closer look at this city in darkness, forgotten by the world. The impression was unforgettable, priceless. It looked as if it was in a state of permanent decay, without beginning and without prospect for an end. The streets were totally empty, while the armored grilles of the shop windows suggested that it was not safe. I have to admit that five years earlier I had the "pleasure" to get to know Bogota— at the time when it was the most dangerous city in the world, when shooting was an inherent part of its nightlife. I tried not to look at the blood, but otherwise it didn't terrify me very much; for the time of my stay I could accept that. It didn't make, however, such a depressing impression as the city of Guayaquil at night. There was some civilization after all; you could work out certain rules giving some sense, or illusion, of predictability. Here, however, there were naked children rummaging in a pile of trash in the middle of the night. I can bear quite a lot, but simply doing anything, even pulling the camera out, was out of the question. I ruled out leaving my bag in the hotel room.

I decided to leave this country as soon as possible. At 7 a.m. I was back at the airport. Because I had no ticket for the further leg of my trip and because it was Sunday, all I could do was to wait for some opportunity. After several hours I was rooted to the spot, having acclimated myself. Thanks to this, I started seeing more than at first glance. I looked closer—but not at the commando squad in front of the entrance—I displayed no particular interest in them. It shocked me, among other things, that virtually all the cars, parking or passing by, were battered, including the police cars. Very interesting subjects of observation were the people themselves. They all had some strange emptiness in their eyes, although in the Third World it's only the elite that visit the airport. Soon I realized that you can recognize the Third World not by the GDP per capita or some other abstract parameter, but by the emptiness in the eyes, by ignorance.

Eventually, after 14 hours of waiting I managed to get out of that country (whose president was soon to become recognized as being mentally ill).

$$*\quad*\quad*$$

The above description is, it has to be emphasized, not representative of South America as a whole. It's a continent of great contrasts with GDP per capita ranging from several hundreds of dollars annually (Bolivia, Guyana) up to Argentina with around $11,000 or even more. Ecuador would be somewhere closer to the bottom end with around $2000. But even this short episode, which ended up in a fiasco, may deliver several interesting reflections, for it is not an exception that in place where once flourished a magnificent civilization, today heaps of trash pile up.

I remember a similar episode when I filmed the Egyptian pyramids at Sakkara. First the frame encompassed the giant construction several thousands of years old, then I fluently passed to a detail in the background, which was the crooked shed of a guard, patched together from uneven pieces of metal sheets, stones, etc.

123

In other words: a fluent pass from the most remote past to modern times, in an absolutely shocking dimension. In such moments it turns out that civilization is not something that just appears and develops automatically. It enables us to look deeper at the events or facts marking the "Axis of the World" and its crowning achievement in the form of the Andean civilization, which I will describe further subsequently.

What really initiated that process? Where did all that knowledge come from? What is left of it? Was there any longterm purpose behind it all?

Only under the influence of such circumstances may we appreciate, for example, the fact that the civilization of Tiahuanaco could have boasted a history spanning over 2000 years. Great, long-term projects were realized, planned for the lifespan of entire generations, which have survived centuries, if not millennia. There had to be some really long-term thought (something that is virtually absent in modern social or political life). I suspect that these people were more conscious of the issue of progress than we are today. Will our "superior" civilization, based on mass culture replacing real information wherever possible, survive at least 200 years? I wouldn't be so sure about that. The fact that such early sophisticated cultures emerged in South America is therefore not only breaking the theory relating to the Bering land bridge, but also the laws governing progress and development. It's a "weird" phenomenon in this respect.

Let's take a closer look then at the other discoveries.

As I mentioned earlier, the evidence supporting the "transpacific" migration theory and the role of Ainuidal people in explaining the origin of American Indians were paradoxically studied mostly in the 1930s and shortly after World War Two, which may explain why this chapter of prehistory is now almost forgotten. One such researcher who gathered quite a lot of materials testifying to such a transpacific migration(s) was an Austrian anthropologist, Robert Heine-Geldern. Along with his assistant, Eckholm, he prepared a special, very evocative exhibition for the International Congress of Americanists (the guys specializing in the prehistory of America), which took place in 1951. Among other things they set up two identical toys, one from Mexico and the other from China. Both portrayed the same animal on wheels, and by the way proved that the ancient Mexicans knew this invention quite well. There were dozens of such set-ups, including identical fishing hooks made of animal bones (one from Easter Island, the other from California), similar weapons, and even musical instruments.

The most important evidence that the Ainu (Ainuidal people) "had something to say" in the Indian case, was, however, yet to come. It was the discovery of a skeleton known as "Kennewick Man." It happened in 1996 in the US state of Washington—on the Pacific coast, naturally. Its age was estimated as approximately 9300 years. One could expect, then, that according to the archaeological time line of this continent, it should reflect anthropologically the first inhabitants pretty well, probably corresponding with the first wave of migration. According to the still "official" theory, it should therefore be a Mongoloid, probably resembling the Inuits (or the Amerindians from eastern Siberia and Alaska, in other words). But that wasn't the case.

It became such a sensation that a reconstruction of the "Kennewick Man's" face even appeared on the covers and front pages of some magazines and newspapers. North American scholars, who forgot about the Ainuidal thread after so many years, were unable to explain the fact that it didn't have typical Indian facial features at all. It was characterized by the dominance of Caucasian features (i.e., of the white race), to such an extent that, on the one hand, Kennewick man was nicknamed by the press as "Patrick Stewart" due to the similarity to the well-known British actor, while on the other hand, the anthropologist who first examined the remains (James Chatters) believed initially that what was found was a skeleton of some modern European settler. Many scientific magazines joined the public dispute, among others *Science* magazine (April 10th, 1998). Unfortunately no DNA analysis was made, because on the basis of a recent law referring to the protection of Indian graves, it had to be buried again shortly after the discovery. On this occasion the press reminded the public that a similar, but even older skeleton—10,675 years old—shared the same fate a couple of years earlier. It was one of the most significant, even famous, revelations on this subject, but of course not the first one of this kind, nor the last! Thus, what I'm trying to present in this book is not a truth based on some single, solitary piece of evidence.

Because of the significance of the finding, it's worth knowing the view of one of the leading US archaeologists in this respect (emphasis by me):

>...the Interior Department released a report by a panel of scientists that said that Kennewick Man could not be linked either to any of modern American Indian tribes or to Europeans. This agreed with Chatters' assessment that he had stood out "from modern American Indians, especially those who occupied Northwestern North America in later prehistory." He was, the panel observed, morphologically closer to *the Ainu of Japan or to Polynesians,* the latter having arrived in the South Pacific much later than Kennewick Man patrolled the Columbia River.[†] Joseph Powell, a member of the panel and a physical anthropologist at the University of New Mexico, said that Kennewick Man "fits into an emerging pattern that these earlier American people are not like the modern people of today."
>
>What light has all this controversy shed so far on the question of who the first Americans were and how and when they got there? That Kennewick Man *looks practically nothing like any contemporary Indian people* is not, on the whole, a very great surprise. None among the handful of skeletal remains from this time period looks much like contemporary Indians either; they tend to look more like southern Asians, it seems. This fits fairly well with what has been surmised from linguistics and mtDNA[††] analysis about the origins of the people who settled the Western Hemisphere.... As Owsley and Jantz have pointed out, this Pacific affinity among our *oldest* skeletons is a pretty good match for the mtDNA haplogroup B, which is common in the Pacific and southern North America, but not in northeastern Siberia or northwestern North

America....

Right now, thanks to developments over the past couple of decades, the number of things we don't know for sure about the initial peopling of this hemisphere exceeds what we do know. Those unknowns will perhaps be resolved one day by the many subfields we have talked about thus far—glacial geology, genetics, linguistics, and so forth—but the real answers about who those were will have to come from the ground. [42]

On the wave of discussion about the origin of this skeleton's "owner," has re-surfaced an even more shocking, but much older, discovery, one forgotten for decades! It was the "Spirit Cave Mummy," also around 9000 years old, being this time a classical mummy of a white man. According to the anthropologist who examined the remains, "they completely do not resemble what we think of when we consider the modern Indians." Once again I will briefly quote the leading American scholars:

Another of those ancient Americans was the Spirit Cave Mummy, which also appeared on the cover of a newsmagazine (Newsweek in April 1999). He was discovered as long ago as 1940 in a rockshelter east of Carson City, Nevada, and was thought at the time to have died about 3000 years ago. Laid to rest in a shallow grave dug into a rockshelter, he had been buried with twined rabbit fur robes and quite sophisticated plaited textiles. Now dated by Riverside to more than 9400 B.P., he is the oldest naturally mummified body in North America and his remains reside in the Nevada State Museum. [42]

All this has triggered such a revolution that many representatives of North American archaeology quite simply rejected the facts, meaning that the conventional theory on the origin of Indians is still, to a large extent, regarded as more or less correct. It turns our knowledge on prehistory upside-down, just like Professor Szalek's discoveries, just like the Monte Verde, as well as what has been described elsewhere in this book. The strange case of "resistance" on the part of North American archaeologists, consisting in the fact that they do not draw conclusions from all this, was commented upon by one of Poland's anthropologists, Dr. Karol Piasecki from the University of Warsaw's Institute of Archaeology:

> It's worth being reminded what consternation was caused [by] the Kennewick Man's discovery. The white man in America 9000 years ago! It not only ruined American stereotypes, but has also triggered the emergence of the absurd conception that the original white population of America was slaughtered by the Asian ancestors of the Indians. No one of those discussants has apparently read the fundamental work by the American anthropologist, E. W. Giford from 1926 on the California Indians, in which are reproduced 19th century photographs of bearded, decidedly white (in the variational sense) Indians. Those Indians, just like the Kennewick Man, are representatives of the so-called Ainuidal (Paleosiberian) race, the archaic form of the white variation, which has survived among the Ainu in Japan and among some California tribes. No wonder—after all, today, in the internet era, reading works older than ten years seems for some to be a completely unnecessary thing. And what if they originated almost 100 years ago….?
>
> The peopling of America is the key problem of American archaeology. With respect to archaeology, political correctness has almost a 100-years' old tradition and consists in adopting the so-called "short history hypothesis." Crossing the Clovis bar, marked by Alex Hrdlicka, was once punished with scientific ostracism; and yet today it's regarded as a proof of outstanding scientific courage. It was perfectly illustrated by the attitude of Tom Dillehay, who long delayed with announcing older datings of part of

128

Top: The Island of the Bird Men as seen from Orongo on Easter Island. Bottom: The quarry at Rano Raraku on Easter Island, where most of the statues were carved. Many are still there.

Top: The largest of the statues, unfinished, at the quarry at Rano Raraku on Easter Island. Below: Igor Witkowski at one of the fallen Moai statues.

Top: Unfinished and unmoved statues at Rano Raraku on Easter Island. Below: Statues that have been re-erected and placed on a platform for modern tourists.

The unusual kneeling statue found at the Rano Raraku quarry site.

Another view of the unusual kneeling statue found at the Rano Raraku quarry site.

Two views of the finely constructed, and seemingly ancient wall of Vinapu on the southeast coast of Easter Island. This is the same kind of construction that is found in South America.

One of the Easter Island moai statues with a red topknot on its head. This silent witness to history is almost as tall as a four-story building!

Two views of the megalithic blocks making up the main Langi on Tonga.

Top: One of the gigantic basalt walls at Nan Madol in Pohnpei Island. Right: An aerial photo of Nan Madol including the coral reef that it sits on which is riddled with tunnels. The dark bay at the top of the photo is a spot where the legendary underwater city of Kanimweiso may be located.

Left: One of the gigantic basalt walls at Nan Madol in Micronesia. Bottom: Underwater columns at Nan Madol, seem to have symbols or writing on them.

Puma Punku—parts of the ruins lie in the former canals (seen here full of rainwater), giving the impression that they were scattered all over the place by some destructive Titans. The bright block in the foreground, thanks to the fractures, shows cross sections of the multi-surface, precise carvings—among others, two "Andean Crosses."

Cut and articulated stone blocks at Puma Punku.

Cut and articulated stone blocks at Puma Punku.

Reconstructed walls at Tiahuanaco.

Cut and articulated stone block at Puma Punku with saw cut and drill holes.

Top: Polychrome vase from Tiahuanaco with the Sun God Kon Tiki Viracocha depicted. Bottom: Disused terraces around Lake Titicaca.

the Monte Verde's findings[†††] The old proverb thus confirms itself—that if facts don't match the theory, …the worse for the facts!"

I, personally, would rather say "ideological correctness." Generally, perception of roots usually has more to do with ideology than with politics.

In a relatively new article, published in *Nature* magazine, Tom Dillehay wrote that: "More recent analyses of the craniofacial features of skulls dating from the end of the Ice Age suggest that the first arrivals were from South Asia or the Pacific Rim." [20, 44]

One can even say that there were two prehistoric migrations of Caucasian people to the Americas: the northern one, tied with the Ainu, with traces in Ecuador and California; and the southern one; whose remains were the "long-eared" from Easter Island as well as certain Indian tribes from South America (described later). The latter interests us much more, however, due to its clear and intriguing "civilizational context" in regard to the "3 peoples = 1 language" empire on the one hand (somewhere in the west) and on the other, the Andean civilizations connected with this "Axis." Such great differences between various groups of Indians cannot be explained even by the fastest evolutionary diversification, which would supposedly take place within 30,000 years or so. There had to be various migrations, from various parts of Asia. It has to be emphasized in this context that *in the history of no other continent are there as many blank spots, even approximately, as in the case of South America.* Let us return then to the beginning and try to trace back this "Axis" across the South Pacific and Indian Oceans.

(Footnotes)
*Present day Turkey.
** In other words, the Finno-Ugric people that we know from Professor Szalek's research and that has left its trace on Easter Island.
*** Supposedly representative of the first Americans.
† I wouldn't be that sure as to the latter.
†† mitochondrial DNA.
††† 33,000 years.

Above: Two bearded figures from Mexican pottery. They completely differ from the images of modern Indians. Note the large, circular decorations in the ears, identical with those described by the first visitors to Easter Island.

Top: A bearded, non-Indian figure of Viracocha from the Peruvian coast (photo: Igor Witkowski). Middle: A reed ship depicted on Peruvian coastal pottery. Below: The simplified bustrophedonic writing discovered near Tiahuanaco by Ibarra -Grasso (The Ibarra-Grasso archive).

131

A bust of the first Chilean Mapuche Indian chief.

An old print of an Inca holding a quipu with writing on his shirt.

Above: An old print of an Inca holding a quipu. Below: A Korean quipu.

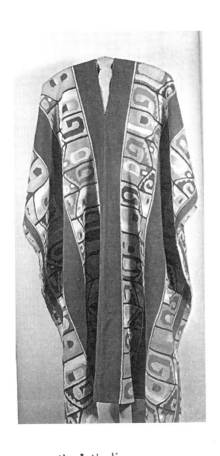

Top: Ancient Peruvian robes that may contain a variation of ancient writing. The symbols contain a large variety of colors, and are repeated very rarely. They may have been a kind of hieroglyphs (photo: Igor Witkowski).Below: The simplified bustrophedonic writing discovered near Tiahuanaco by Ibarra-Grasso (The Ibarra-Grasso archive).

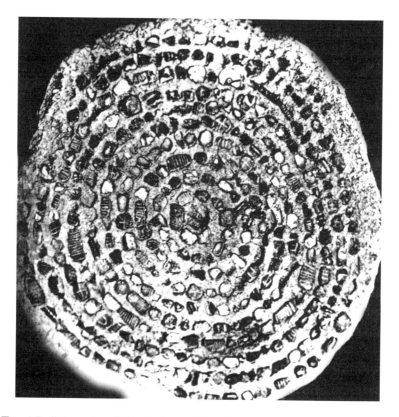

Top: A Bolivian priest, Pedro de Acosta from Oruro province, discovered (some sixty years ago) that his parishioners recorded the biblical commandments in this a peculiar way. It's a clay plate around 60 cm (2") in diameter, in which colored stones were fixed. Later, the leading Venezuelan archaeologist, Jose Cruxent discovered such a system of writing, further north. (The Escomel Archive).Below: The noblemen in Polynesia and in the Andes used the same, unusual decorations in their hair. Easter Island glyph on the left and Indus Valley on the right. (P. Herrmann).

5

THE CHAIN OF TRACES

Let's start from the west, from the center of the Indus Valley civilization, mentioned in Chapter Two describing Professor Szalek's work. That's where the entire process started.

The main centers of the Indus Valley civilization were some of the most sophisticated and oldest metropolises of the ancient world: Mohenjo Daro and Harappa. These cities are also nicknamed the "Hiroshima and Nagasaki of the ancient world." This results from the fact that when at the beginning of the 1950s excavating archaeologists reached the level of former streets, they found skeletons scattered all over the cities, sometimes in strange poses, even holding hands. It seemed as if suddenly the cities were struck by some strange cataclysm. This is worth noting, because a similar scene is visible in the case of Puma Punku, presented in the final chapter! The skeletons are rated among the most radioactive in the world, equal to the ones gathered from the ruins of Hiroshima and Nagasaki. Soviet scientists working there after World War Two, in an excavation site nearby, unearthed skeletons whose radioactivity exceeds the norm by 50 times! Mohenjo Daro became famous also for its mysterious shapeless lumps—thousands of them—known as "the black stones." There is a presumption that these are remains of pottery, or more likely just clumps of bricks, which have partially melted under the influence of a very high temperature, around 1400-1600 °C (2550-2910 °F). The centers of both cities bear the traces of an explosion, or at least something resembling one; the buildings are literally leveled, and the better their condition is, the further they are from the centers. Other even more telltale ruins were found in this area too. Between the Ganges River and the Rajmahal Mountains, archaeologists found ruins of a city with clear traces of extremely high temperatures acting on them, with huge masses of bricks and pieces of walls that are sintered together, their surfaces vitrified to a substance resembling volcanic

137

glass. The same was observed in the downtowns of Hiroshima and Nagasaki. After the first nuclear test in the New Mexico desert, the sand close to the explosion site was also sintered and partially melted, and formed a new mineral named "Trinitite," after the code name of the test: "Trinity." A similar mineral was later found also in Iran, Peru, Turkey, France, Scotland and Ireland, although it would require careful examination to rule out the possibility that it is material of meteorite origin. As far as I know, no sensible alternative explanation has been proposed by scholars.

One of the co-designers of the first American nuclear bombs was Robert Oppenheimer. He had earlier studied Sanskrit, among other languages, so he knew Hindu books in their original language, not "contaminated" by incompetent modern translations. He summarized the first nuclear test with a quotation from the *Mahabharata,* one of these ancient Sanskrit books: "I have unleashed the power of the Universe, now I became the destroyer of worlds." When he was asked later—in 1952 during a press conference at Rochester University—whether the test near Alamogordo was the first ever carried out, he answered: "Yes..." adding after a while, "in our times."[21]

Mohenjo Daro was discovered in 1922 by an officer of the British Archaeological Survey of India, R. D. Banerji, shortly after the discovery of the Harappa ruins around 590 km to the north. Before the war large excavations were initiated, but without the stratigraphic approach used presently. The last major excavation project there was carried out by Dr. G. F. Dales from 1964 to 1965, after which excavations were banned due to problems conserving the exposed structures from erosion. In the 1980s the last major research project was completed, but without excavating. German and Italian survey teams generated extensive architectural documentation, combined with detailed surface surveys, surface scraping and probing. It was led by Dr. Michael Jansen (RWTH) and Dr Maurizio Tosi.

According to modern knowledge, both Mohenjo Daro and Harappa experienced their "glory days" between 2500 and 1500 years B.C. (4500—3500 years ago). One can confidently say that what Tiahuanaco was for both Americas, Mohenjo Daro was for the south-Asian cultures. They were, by the way, probably the largest metropolises of the contemporary world, housing—it is estimated—around 35,000 people in each case.

Even a brief glimpse at the excavation site, or the site map, discloses that both Mohenjo Daro and Harappa were centers of an unbelievably highly developed civilization. The buildings were constructed from fired bricks in a relatively modern way and according to a city plan approved before construction begun. It was, speaking frankly, something completely unbelievable in ancient times and even today it's not that common at all in the local, provincial towns.

Apart from complexes resembling military barracks, and centrally located large buildings—sometimes three stories high—probably for public use, there were of course residential buildings as well. These came in full variety, from very small ones with only one room, through residences having more than one storey and even a dozen rooms, up to large tenement houses, probably for many families. In the trade and craft district were rows of various shops and workshops for pottery, textiles, dyeing, handicrafts, metallurgy, etc. The base of the city's existence was, however, agriculture, in the valley of the fertile river. In every building there was (believe it or not!) a bathroom, or at least a water closet. Mohenjo Daro and Harappa had such sophisticated, well-planned and built-in-advance sewage and water supply systems, that they were in many cases superior to the respective systems functioning today in the Pakistani or Indian towns in the vicinity (both cities are presently in Pakistan—Mohenjo Daro in the south, around 200 km north of Haidarabad, and Harappa in the north, some 20 km west from the city of Sahiwal).

The streets crossed each other at straight angles and they were, among other things, the first streets covered with (a naturally occurring) asphalt. The Indus Valley civilization maintained trade and exchange with the neighboring kingdoms. It probably had an entire fleet of trade ships; caravans were used on the land routes. There is a widespread conviction that this civilization didn't develop "from scratch," but appeared there more or less already formed, for apparently it didn't adopt foreign influences. This doesn't surprise us.

Many researchers point out the fact that some traces of an

ancient advanced civilization were also found to the south, on islands in the Indian Ocean, Ceylon (today's Sri Lanka), and the Maldives—as if the culture "radiated" southward. Thor Heyerdahl described these traces as early as the 1950s, [22] and later David Hatcher Childress presented a lot of evidence in one of his books.[21] No wonder; after all, it's these islands that mark the beginning of the "sea track" that leads eventually to the Pacific.

In fact however, the first puzzling findings were made in Ceylon in the second half of the 19th century in the form of petroglyphs. A young British officer of the colonial forces, Percy Fawcett, came to the conclusion that the mysterious signs engraved in the mountains, on rocks, are part of some ancient Tibetan writing named "Sansar" which preceding the known writing, Sanskrit. It was supposedly discovered in a Tibetan monastery in 1845 and considered "very old." The French missionary who allegedly was the author of this discovery, Abbé Huc, claimed that it originated from some sunken land or continent, inhabited by an ancient race of wise men. I didn't manage to get to copies of any of these signs, but a comparison with the Mohenjo Daro writing or confirmation of the Tibetan thread would be quite interesting.

In 1879 another Frenchman, Louis Jacolliot, published a book containing Hindu myths, including, among other analogous legends, a story about such a lost land and the "Ruta people" which was said to thrive there. One such Hindu source is the great mythical or religious epic called the *Ramayana*, probably dating back as far as the 21st century B.C. It describes some "land of the gods," ruled by Rama, which was said to be "the middle of the world," surrounded by oceans.

Another interesting milestone in the Indian Ocean, slightly further from the Indian subcontinent than is Ceylon, is the small archipelago of the Maldives. It begins some 300 km (200 miles) south of India and stretches south, containing around 1200 islands, mostly very small, with the combined area of only 300 sq. km. According to the prevailing notion, there was never any indigenous civilization in the ancient times, although after World War Two a strange artifact was found. Scientists unearthed, among other things, an unusual stone statue portraying a man with elongated ears. This "long eared" man attracted the attention of the famous researcher studying migration tracks in the Indian and Pacific oceans, Thor Heyerdahl, who later wrote a book on these discoveries entitled *The Maldives Mystery*. It's an important clue, if not also a kind of lodestar, marking a clear trace to the east, almost as if it was a kind of starting point. It has to be emphasized again that the "long eared" did not occur only on Easter Island:

1. In India it was the attribute of the *rulers* and divine figures such as the Buddha and the saints;
2. Then they occur in the Maldives;
3. The *ruling class* in the Marquesas Islands, to the west of Easter Island, in the Pacific, shared this custom of elongating ears;
4. Then it appears as the "symbol of isolation," according to academic science, on Easter Island;
5. The Incas (who were actually the kings and members of the aristocracy of the Andean empire which called itself "Tahuantinsuyu") were also clearly familiar with elongated ears. There is, for example, a woodcut from the time of the Spanish conquest reproduced in this book which portrays "the long eared, white Inca." Also their main god— Viracocha—was often portrayed with long ears, with something like large balls inserted in holes in the earlobes, like giant, ball-shaped earrings. I personally saw around a dozen such proofs in the museums of the Peruvian capital, Lima, as well as their equivalents of the "bird-men," allegedly unique to Easter Island. One couldn't imagine a clearer link proving the transpacific migration and distant roots of the American civilizations. Of course, as I mentioned, it doesn't occur to the scholars studying it at all! The evidence given by the numerous sculptures and woodcuts portraying the Peruvian "long eared" people are supplemented by written descriptions, such as the one by Pedro de Cieza de Leon, presented below.

141

As far as the Incas are concerned, there is even an indusputible trace in the bi-ethnical character of the state, i.e., the aristocracy represented a different race from the rest of the nation. Later on I present evidence that also demonstrates that they used *two different languages* on certain occasions; one was known by the rulers only and was used for religious purposes. It directly resembles the strange social system known from Easter Island, as if it was just transferred further east and north.

Contrary to what the attitude of scholars suggests (or rather, their *lack* of attitude), there is really no shortage of historical traditions shedding light on various aspects of this phenomenon. One of them was left by the early Spanish chronicler, Pedro de Cieza de Leon:

> The Indians always considered as members of the aristocracy the people who lived in two places within the city, called Anancuzco and Orincuzco,* and even some Indians wanted to say that the first Inca must have been from one of these lines; and the other — from the second one; but I'm not sure of what the *long ears* say, nor what has been *written*. 23

Another chronicler, from the 19th century, and therefore presenting a later, less clear picture, Adolph Bandelier, questioned locals from the vicinity of Tiahuanaco regarding their form of social organization and the ethnic divisions within their community:

> The reply came that there were only two [divisions]: Arasaya and Masaya. These two groups are geographically divided at the village. The Masaya occupy the building south, Arasaya those north, of the central square, the dividing line going ideally through the center of the plaza from east to west. This geographical division is (at Tiahuanaco) even indicated at church. We saw, when at mass, the principals of the two clusters, each with his staff of office, entering in procession. 49

142

Let me state it clearly once again: this all proves that the most sophisticated civilizations of South America were just an offshoot, "planted" there consciously, of a greater civilization that is now completely forgotten. All the fundamental cultural heritage was simply transferred there from outside. There must have been a relatively far-reaching plan and a great deal of thought involved! One of the most striking circumstances in this case is that—despite the overall time span of thousands of years and tremendous distances—the most important features of this heritage, such as the writing, had not been changed during the process! That's quite unbelievable, to put it bluntly, for it shatters all contemporary theories of migration, diffusion, the spreading of cultures, and so on. Science would have to revolutionize itself if it were to incorporate such facts into its machinery. It's not the first, nor the last, example presented in this book that shows that the "Axis" is something contradicting our understanding of history, but that it is also "tied" with no less important "curiosities" from fields other than geography alone. After all the Axis isn't anything local; with South America it encompasses more than half of the Earth's circumference and reaches back to the very beginnings of civilization.

But lets go back again, briefly, to the Maldives.

Thor Heyerdahl made several priceless observations which led him to other remains of this extinct culture. Assuming that, as throughout the Pacific, a special role should be attributed to the Sun cult, he took an interest in a tiny island, Fua Mulaku, lying precisely on the equator. It paid off, for he found there some remains, probably ruins of a shrine connected with the Sun cult (during the equinoxes, twice a year, the Sun passes precisely in zenith). The remaining walls bore a striking similarity to the stone platforms from Polynesia, first and foremost from Easter Island. The walls were made from polygonal, many-sided blocks, closely fitting each other—almost like those found in the high Andes.

He also heard a local legend about "the ancient Redin people," known for long time in the Maldives. The legend had it that the first inhabitants of the archipelago were some tall people, coming from afar, with white skin.[21] It was they who supposedly built the

143

temples.

Graham Hancock mentioned this tradition, conveyed to him by a scholar from the Maldives National Institute for Linguistic and Historical Research. The Redin people were supposedly (emphasis by me):

> ...*very tall*. They were fair-skinned, and they had brown hair, *blue eyes* sometimes. And they were very, very good at sailing. So this story has been around in Maldives for many, many years, and there are certain places where they say the Redin camped here, and certain places which they say here the Redin were buried. But we don't really know how old or how long ago it happened....
>
> The Redin came *long before* any other Maldivians. Between them and the present population other people had also come, but none were as potent as the Redin, and there were many of them. They not only used sail but also oars, and therefore moved with great speed at sea... [43]

Further east, in the Pacific, there is of course no shortage of mysterious ruins, best described in the book *Lost Cities of Ancient Lemuria and the Pacific* by David Hatcher Childress. I will mention only the most important ones here, starting from the western edge of this ocean.

Around 700 miles (or slightly more than 1000 km) to the northeast of the Australian coast lies the island of New Caledonia, being an overseas possession of France. In the 1960s the director of the local museum, Luc Chevalier, found certain peculiar structures, mounds, which—as it was about to turn out—did not fit any existing academic scheme. They are made from sand and gravel up to 7-10 feet high (2-3 m) and up to 300 ft. in diameter. Chevalier counted over 400 of them. They occur in the southern part of New Caledonia, as well as on the small Pine Island nearby. What seemed rather strange was that the mounds were essentially deprived of any vegetation. Soon after the discovery, four of them were subjected to excavation; Chevalier suspected that they were burial sites, as was the case in Europe with Neolithic mounds. However, no graves were found; instead, in their centers were cylinders made of something resembling concrete! The material consisted of ground limestone and seashells, and as such resembled rather the concrete used on a small scale by the Romans. Radiocarbon dating only made the findings more obscure, for the sequence of dates ranged from around 7000 years ago, up to 13000 years B.P! This contradicted, once again, the official theory of migrations in the Pacific basin. This part of the Pacific supposedly was populated as late as 5000 years ago, although it doesn't seem logical; after all, nearby Australia was reached by the first incomers almost ten times earlier.

The dispersion of dates indicates on the other hand a continuity of population, which means that for millennia this territory was under the influence of one and the same culture, which resembles the Protodravidian scheme (see for example the Jomon, the Tarim Basin or the durability of the writing). The existence of processed and ground limestone (concrete) also forces scholars to re-evaluate their knowledge, for according to the official canon, concrete was invented at the turn of the 2nd and 3rd centuries in the Roman Empire (although initially it was very weak, used mostly in road construction, bridges, and so on).

Usually there was just one such cylinder in a mound's base, but in one of them Chevalier found two. They had diameters from 3 ft. to 6.5 ft. (1–1.9 m) and were from 3 to 6 ft. high (1–1.9 m).[21]

We move further east…

In the central part of the Pacific lies the Polynesian archipelago of Tonga. It's one of few places in this region which wasn't colonized by Europeans, although it's the remains from older times that are the most interesting; they are quite peculiar and unusual, if not even puzzling. There is, on the island named Eua to be precise, the only stone trilithion known in Polynesia: an arc resembling the Greek letter Π. It's known as the "Trilithion of Ha'amonga." It consists of two pillars, each almost 5 m high (or 16 ft.), and weighing around 50 tons, as well as a horizontal "bar." It wouldn't be anything strange if it were not for the fact that trilithions constitute a standard of Neolithic construction in

145

Europe where they are particularly abundant in Scotland and on the Atlantic coast of France. The term "Neolithic" is associated generally with something ancient, to put it gently.

It may not be any proof of such connections, but among other things it calls to mind another such case from South America. When I was in Argentina in 1997, as one of the points in my itinerary consisting of rarely visited places, was a site that is known as Tafi del Valle. It's situated northwest of Buenos Aires, in the foothills of the Andes, close to the western border with Chile. It is a remote place even by Argentina standards, and just as in the case of Easter Island, it's something that doesn't fit the scheme of isolation. There, in a mountain park, one finds a kind of megalithic ceremonial center (*mega lithos* means "big stones," and thus signifies the epoch when people expressed their notions mostly in great stones, or worshipped them as embodiments of divine forces, the *Neolithic*). The Argentine site wouldn't be anything unusual either, if not for the fact that it looked as if all the characteristic elements from Neolithic Europe were transferred there, as if by some magic force. I found in this case :

1. Trilithions, which were usually cardinal points in astronomical observations;
2. Stone circles, made probably for the same purpose;
3. Phalluses, or portrayals of erected penises, which were the symbols of fertility (by the way, often covered by ornaments suggesting that they practiced extensive tattooing of this part of the body).

There were virtually no differences. It all looked the same — nothing lacked, nor was there anything unknown from the Old Continent; the only difference was that the "specimens" were generally smaller. It seemed peculiar to me, astounding, but at that time I couldn't make the connection with the other facts yet, the facts which proved that indeed there must have been a certain "line of communication" in ancient times, as the case of the Gallehus horn versus the Easter Island writing alone suggests. Perhaps the trilithion from Tonga is also a manifestation of the same phenomenon?

Generally it's something strange if you get to the other end of the world and find the same set of cultural symbols. It suggests among other things that their religion was identical, for the symbols reflect specific practices or customs.

In the case of the trilithion from Tonga, it's validated also by the fact that on top of the "bar" there are small holes, as if for placing some sticks or stones, just as if indeed it was a kind of astronomical tool. In those times astronomy was part of religion in such a sense that celestial bodies were divine and the natural cycles symbolized the divine order. As I have mentioned, we still find a shadow of these times in the form of certain holidays: Christmas was originally the winter solstice holiday, and Easter the spring equinox holiday, symbolizing rebirth of nature; plus Monday as the day of the Moon, Sunday, the day of the Sun, Saturday as the day of Saturn, and so on. It is common knowledge that the cult of the Sun was practiced in the Indus Valley, throughout the Pacific, and in the Andes as well.

There is one more such proof in Tonga, connecting Polynesia with South America. On the grounds of the local Tongatapu fortress (or perhaps religious center?) there is a stone platform which resembles a "flattened" truncated pyramid, reduced to a four-layer platform. It resembles the Easter Island platform, Ahu Vinapu, through the curved sides of its blocks. Once again it also resembles walls attributed to the Incas in the Andes.

This platform, known as Langi Tauhala, surprises one with the size of its blocks (by the way: in the Andes they sometimes used curved, polygonal blocks weighing up to 100–200 tons). The largest of them is 7.4 m long (24 ft.), 2.2 m wide (7 ft.) and is around 1.5 ft. (or 45 cm) thick. The entire wall of which it's a part is 222 m long—almost 730 ft. As we could guess, it would be hard to find any oral tradition in the memory of the locals which could give us any clue as to the identity of the builders; it reminds me of the situation with Tiahuanaco, in Bolivia. When one of the first Spanish chroniclers asked the Indians if it was they who built it, they answered with a smile that they found the ruins when they arrived there, long ago.

Peculiar ruins, not matching any common scheme, were also

found on another island, this time in the Kiribati archipelago located roughly mid-point between Hawaii and Australia. They were described by Erich von Däniken, the famous Swiss researcher, after he received a letter from a former missionary living in South Africa, in the book titled *Reise nach Kiribati (Trip to Kiribati)*. He mentioned, among other things, some large, ancient graves— supposedly graves of the giants—which should attract our attention in the light of earlier information on the Protodravidians (known in this context as the Protopolynesians).

In his second letter the missionary described them more precisely:

> We became aware of the strange and hard to explain ancient history of these islands, soon after we learned their language… The first thing which struck me was the fact that the islanders had two names for the people. They called themselves "aomata," which means just "humans." Every one with a white skin and tall was however named "te-i-matang," which in literal translation means "man from the land of gods." When we got to know them better, we found that a similar difference between locals and strangers occurs on all the islands.

I observe that white people were classified in a similar way in various parts of the world, including practically the entirety if Polynesia, as well as Southern and Central America. In Polynesia the first European visitors were granted respect (as long as they gave no reason to be treated otherwise) as "gold-haired children of Tangaroa," the god who according to their traditions came millennia before as a teacher and civilizer.

The same was apparently the case in the Americas. As we know, in Central America the Spaniards were initially treated as gods, as the messengers of Quetzalcoatl or Kukulcan. The first Spanish troops that landed on the coast of Tahuantinsuyu (in what is today southern Ecuador) could venture deep into the foreign territory of the empire because the local Incan commanders were not that keen to take responsibility for mounting an assault against the "Viracochas." If that myth of "superhuman," white-skinned beings was so strong and important, and so common, then we cannot assume that it wasn't somehow anchored in reality. It's worth remembering that mythologies almost unanimously describe the land of the tall, white people as the land of the gods at the same time: the Hindu *Ramayana*, the legends of the Hopi Indians, and the traditions of the Pacific peoples. I sometimes wonder if these beings were not akin to the so-called "Nordics" of UFO contactee lore (not to be confused with people from Scandinavia); but that's a tangential remark. In any case, archaeology has so far not managed to explain this notion, this attitude; nor has it explained the unbelievably high level of both the Mohenjo Daro and the Tiahuanaco civilizations. It's worth remembering in this context that for the contemporaries it was obvious, and they repeated, as if for future generations, that this progress was the product of beings which did come "from heaven."

After this digression lets go back to Kiribati. What did von Däniken find?

As he himself wrote, the information offered by the missionary turned out to be correct, although he did not hide his disappointment that he expected to find all this in better condition. The alleged grave of a giant was 5.3 m long—over 17 ft! Among the stones described by the missionary was a stone compass, being indeed a sort of signpost pointing out the other Polynesian islands; he also found two blocks made of granite, a mineral not occurring on Kiribati. Two others were also made of rocks "imported" from afar.

The area lacking any vegetation was found, as it turned out, to be only 14 m in diameter. In the middle there was a square, framed by the stones, with sides 5.1 m long (16 ft. 8in.). It was the only structure visible there. Von Däniken wanted to test the place for radioactivity, and hence a Geiger-Müller meter was turned on, but no unusual radiation was detected. When his assistant, Willy, attempted to enter the square with the device, he was stopped by the local guide, who claimed that the "spirits" would not tolerate any foreign life there and birds were seen dying when flying over the square. One more mystery of the Pacific thus remained unsolved.

Much more valuable discoveries were made on other islands,

149

named Malden and Upolu, lying in the Samoa archipelago to the southeast. According to some researchers, what has been found there provides the strongest testimony for the hypothesis concerning some lost land being the cradle of the Pacific civilization.

The former rector of the University of New Zealand, John MacMillan Brown, described the island extensively in his book entitled *The Riddle of the Pacific*. According to him, numerous stone platforms and stepped pyramids were found there, up to 9 m (or 30 ft. high), as well as roads, lined up with basalt, which lead... straight into the ocean! The roads connect the pyramids and then disappear into the ocean floor! What is most intriguing, however, is that on the continuation of one of them, *at a distance of over 1000 miles,* there is another island, named Rarotonga *on which an identical road descends right into the ocean.* It's a legendary stone road known as Ara Metua and as was ascertained, it's the oldest such construction in all of Polynesia—unless older ones still are hidden under the waves. There are also identical pyramidal platforms, such as on Upolu, which confirms the theory that these islands (which certainly were tips of a larger Pacific land in the Ice Age) were once the abode of some significant culture, parts of one cultural circle. By the way, the pyramids and platforms are very similar to those on the coast of Peru (the Moche culture) and in Central America. Of course, they also resemble the stone platforms from Easter Island.

But regardless of the importance of these findings, there is no more interesting place in the Pacific than Nan Madol and the ruins on the adjacent, smaller islands. In fact, Nan Madol lies on the island of Pohnpei (previously known as Ponape) which is just a link in a larger chain of islands bearing exotic names: Yap, Ngulu, Eauripik, Pulap, Truk, Oroluk, Nukuoro and Kosrae. They all form the Federated States of Micronesia, except for Kosrae which is actually an independent state. For us, however, it is Pohnpei and Kosrae that are the most interesting.

The local ruins are unique on a world-wide scale, and along with the other places forming the "Axis" (with Puma Punku in the forefront) rank among the most mysterious. What is most unusual, especially in reference to Pohnpei/Ponape is that:

150

1. Undoubtedly it is the largest such complex in the entire Pacific basin, being the size of a large ancient city;
2. Part of it lies underwater, and that a considerable depth, which clearly suggests that it may date back as far as the last glaciation, some 12,000 years ago, however strange that may seem;
3. Just as in the case of Puma Punku (near Tiahuanaco, to be described in the final chapter), the present inhabitants have no idea as to who built it, nor what they built it for;
4. The method of construction is quite strange, it's not made of cut stones, but mostly of naturally crystallized long basalt columns, which are hexagonal;
5. Streets are replaced by water canals and there are even underwater tunnels connecting some ruins. Because the presently accessible part has a "reasonable" water level (water is only in the canals, the buildings are not flooded), it suggests that various parts were built in various times, taking into account the rising sea level (i.e., the accessible part is the most recently constructed). The whole scenario obviously makes investigating the roots of this place almost impossible, as far as ascertaining its true age. Then there is the fact that it lies in the tropics, which means that there is hardly any trace of so-called "perishable artifacts" (although bones were found).

But let's start from the ruins on the nearby island of Kosrae.

The locals named these ruins "Insaru" and they are known as "the city of the kings." They are also built from hexagonal blocks. Some of them have a mass of 30–60 tons, however, which is the equivalent of a typical tank, or half of a locomotive. Usually they are uncut, I mean unfinished, but in some instances they display signs that precise treatment and finishing weren't foreign to the builders. As you can imagine, scholars, apart from Professor

151

Szalek, have no idea as to who these builders were.

A couple of hundred kilometers to the west of Kosrae lies the other of the two strange islands: Pohnpei/Ponape. It is situated more or less north of the line connecting New Guinea with Hawaii, closer to New Guinea, approximately one third of the distance. Its relative remoteness from the larger land masses only deepens the mystery of the origin of the ruins found here. Circumstances could have been slightly different during the last glaciation, however, for Indochina was much "longer" and approached the enlarged Solomon Islands. Only a distance of about 1000 km divided it from Pohnpei. One may even have the impression that Pohnpei was a kind of "springboard" for the conquest of the great ocean.

Supposedly the original name of the island, given by the locals—Pohnpei—means "on the altar," which suggests that it served some religious or ceremonial purpose, as was often the case with centers of ancient cultures. "Ponape," by the way, was a German name from the times when it was their colony.

Nan Madol occupies very large area for an ancient city (the part that's now on the surface): 28 square kilometers or around 11 square miles. The central part of the complex consists of around a hundred artificially formed islets, and occupies an area of one square mile (2.5 km^2), on which are situated the remains of various buildings made of the aforementioned basalt blocks, having masses of up to 20 tons, some weighing even 40–50 tons. They are very similar to those on Kosrae, where they probably were transported from Pohnpei, for basalt does not occur on that island. The larger ones are connected by tunnels. Probably the most important part of this complex is the funeral sector, the "royal mortuary islet," to be specific, which is called Nan Dowas. Here, walls 18 to 25 feet high surround a central tomb enclosure within the main courtyard. The excavations that have been carried out there provided results which were shocking for scholars (but not for us!) and have been described elsewhere.

The first to carry out archaeological research in Nan Madol were the Germans before the First World War, but even before that there was a Pole, named Jan Stanislaw Kubary, who contributed to the unraveling of this ruins' riddle. He was quite a mysterious figure, and although various points of information indicate that he might have made some valuable findings, we cannot say anything specific about it. The fact is that he was quite obsessed about this place, in the positive sense, for it was a place completely unknown then, before the end of the 19ᵗʰ century. According to his own announcements, he collected quite a lot of various artifacts over the years, and prepared them for shipment to Europe, but the ship transporting this precious cargo sank near the Marshall Islands.

Kubary was apparently so depressed by this that he committed suicide, and therefore his findings are only the subject of legend, although nobody can be really sure about the reason for his death. No wonder that it initiated legends about a curse that supposedly "guarded" this strange place in some way, legends that were augmented by the fact that all of Kubary's records and notes, left at his home, also perished in an "accidental" fire in the 1930s.[21] This thread unfortunately continued to develop in later years, for he wasn't the last person who died in mysterious circumstances, or was lost and never found. Even relatively recently one can count dozens of people who shared this doom. More on this later.

After him, the work in Nan Madol was continued by an outstanding German archaeologist, Dr. Paul Hambruch. Most of the currently extant plans and maps are his work. It took him over fifteen years. No major research work was carried out in the 1920s and 1930s, but during World War Two the Japanese probably excavated part of the cemetery (in fact they started before the war), but the resulting material was supposedly destroyed in the course of war operations. Anyway, the results of their efforts are not known. In effect, despite numerous efforts, very little hard data was obtained about this place and the fundamental questions are still left unanswered.

One of the first publications to shed some light on the site, or rather just presented the first comprehensive descriptions of the place to the public, was a book published in Germany in 1939 by a then-popular German traveler and writer, Herbert Rittlinger, titled *Der masslose Ozean (The Immeasurable Ocean)*. The information presented caused a lot of commotion, but was correct, based probably on Hambruch's research. He was the first who described the underwater part of Nan Madol, with stone roads on the ocean's floor, and the local legends saying that once it was a capital of a

153

large and rich kingdom. He also described some metal tablets that were found in the ruins and were covered with some unknown writing.

This interesting thread was picked up by Erich von Däniken, who ventured an expedition to Nan Madol. It was described in his book *The Gold of the Gods*. What is most interesting is that he mentions certain previoiusly unknown results of the Japanese searches, which had nothing to do with scientific research. According to him, they were simply looking for treasure and rare metals needed for the war industry which were supposed to be there. One of these was platinum, and according to the locals, the most significant figures buried in Nan Dowas were enclosed hermetically in coffins made of that metal. Von Däniken himself was not sure as to the authenticity of this story, but he quoted certain data which confirmed that indeed during the war this precious metal began to be exported from Pohnpei, although it does not occur there in any natural deposits. Von Däniken based his story to a large extent on the account of the aforementioned Rittlinger, who claimed that the Japanese continued this practice until two of their divers were lost during such mission, for the coffins were located underwater.

The unusual emergence of platinum, and its role, is of course a strange and unexplained fact, for this metal is very difficult to handle. It's very rare and melts at a very high temperature, around 1773°C (much higher even than in the case of steel, around 1540°C, let alone copper 1083°C). But we should bear in mind that despite that, it was apparently crucial in places along certain paths, for it was used by the Jomon of Japan, in Ecuador and in the empire of the Incas as well. It's all the more strange in that, according to official science, the builders of Nan Madol were Stone Age people.

The occurrence of platinum in these civilizations is something that breaks existing rules in general. It's enough to take into account that when the Spaniards reached the treasure troves of the Incas, which was during the period of the advanced Renaissance in Europe, they had no idea what it was. Because it was very foreign to them—they were unable to process it—they coined the word "platina" (for "plata"—silver), which was a rather contemptuous epithet, something like "little silver," meaning that it resembled silver but was effectively useless for them. In this context it would be extremely interesting to know how the Incas were able to generate such a high temperature (and the Ainu, and in all probability the inhabitants of Nan Madol); it was a metallurgy far in advance of the European or Arabic metallurgy of these times. The Soviet mathematician and researcher of the so-called "palaeocontacts," and a member of the Soviet Academy of Sciences, Vladimir Avinskiy, used to call such a cases *"historically incompatible technicisms,"* for they were anomalously far in advance of the general level of technology for the epoch in which they occurred. It's not the only such example of anomalies emerging along the Axis.

The other interesting thread that comes out from the scarce information pertaining to the Japanese searches is that they were finding abnormally large human bones.[21] Such information was supposedly published by them before the outbreak of the war. It indicated that the builders, or the ruling class to be precise, were over 2 meters tall (over 6 ft. 7 in.). It reminds me of the description and photograph of one of the Tarim Valley mummies, nicknamed "the Yingpan Man." He measures precisely 2 meters.[46] The outbreak of war made verification of these Japanese reports impossible, although I found an article in one of our popular magazines, which describes the searches (mostly for treasures!) carried out on Pohnpei in the 1950s and 1960s. I quote short fragments:

> …In the southern part, an underground tunnel with a crypt and altar were discovered, which brings forth associations with altars in Christian churches. *A human skeleton was found in the crypt.* After careful examination it turned out that it was *2.3 m long* and [the body] weighed 135 kg*. Anthropologists have formulated a thesis on its *European* origin. Melvin Norris, during inspection of the crypt, has observed strange flashes resembling lights of atmospheric discharges.
>
> The searches for the treasure began in the

155

summer of 1956. Captain John Gilbertson from Auckland turned to experts with a request for an assessment of a cross found in Nan Madol. Detailed examination dated it back to around 300 year A.D. The gold, from which the object was made, was of amazing purity, which in connection with its priceless historical value has caused large interest in the cross. The authorities of New Zealand proposed Gilbertson the sum of 15,000 dollars for the cross, but eventually the transaction did not take place. News of the marvelous cross has spread around the world like a lightning's flash. Collectors and hobbyists alike from various parts of the world conducted negotiations in this case. Eventually the American William Messner became its buyer—for the sum of $40,000, after which he donated it to a museum in Philadelphia. When journalists wanted to interview him after the transaction, it turned out that he sailed into the sea, on his boat, and no trace of him was ever found. [45]

A later section of the article is abundant in descriptions of people or expeditions which were lost in the ruins of Nan Madol itself, or after carrying out explorations there. The author has counted over 200 such people, all of whom perished in mysterious circumstances. In some cases even large, well prepared teams shared this fate. For example:

Two schooners with a crew of 17 vanished on their way to Nan Madol, no traces of them whatsoever were ever found. A ship with four British and two Australians, being close to Nan Madol, transmitted a "May Day" signal. In spite of the rescue, sent immediately, the crew nor the ship were never found... In June of 1970 three expeditions started their searches for treasure. Two days later four men swam to the adjacent island in a state of extreme exhaustion. They were the only survivors from the

teams which counted 26 men. The remaining 22
have just vanished!

The fame of the mysterious ruins became so great that it
eventually attracted the most renowned scientist working on
Pacific cultures (if not the best of them all), and an author of
excellent books, Professor John MacMillan Brown from New
Zealand. He prepared an expedition for seven months, gathering
and analyzing various materials. He never made it, however; he
was found dead in his office. At the moment of his death he was
47 years old and was completely healthy. The cause of his death
could not be explained.

The aforementioned Jan Kubary also fell victim to the "curse,"
in 1907. And the German governor of Ponape died in his sleep
after a trip to the ruins.

It may be, of course, just a chain of strange coincidences (but
dozens of them?), but it also may be that there is simply something
on that island that has not been discovered yet, and is not *supposed*
to be discovered. According to one of the legends, there is some
unknown underground part of the complex, and it's the mysterious,
not fully explored tunnels, which lead there.

One of the main objectives of the few post-war scientific
groups which worked there was the ascertaining of Nan Madol's
age. The results remain unclear, however.

In the 1960s an expedition sent by the American Smithsonian
Institution got there, but facing the overall scale of the complex
and unfavorable climatic conditions, it only touched the very
surface of this place. In effect, the results were far from conclusive.
Datings of some layers of ash were made, for example, achieving
the age of 900–1000 years, and on this basis this age, almost
automatically, was attributed to the entire ruins. It turned out to be
wrong because, for instance, the latter (1970s) thermo-luminescent
dating of the pottery gave very different results—at least 2000
years, which itself contradicts the official theories on the peopling
of the Pacific. Of course the greatest challenge to these claims
lies on the ocean's floor: the existence of a certain part of the city
which has probably been flooded for millennia, suggesting in turn
that Nan Madol has quite a long history indeed. But we may only

scratch the surface in this respect.

One of the interesting questions raised by the phenomenon of Nan Madol refers to the methods of its construction. As we know, the weight of certain blocks is counted in the dozens of tons and in this respect the ruins are comparable with the Great Pyramid of Egypt. How were such large masses transported and piled up to construct walls over 30 feet high (10 m)? David Hatcher Childress—author of a book on the mysteries of the Pacific (among others)—writes that he heard a legend there, according to which the complex was built by two brothers with the help of some "flying dragon." Another legend says that the blocks were moved and raised by the power of magic.

Rubbish? Perhaps it only proves that the locals knew nothing about the remains of something that was beyond their imagination? Perhaps, however, some unknown forces were indeed used by the mysterious, omnipotent race. One thing is certainly striking here, and that is the use of "magical power," like the "mana" spoken of on Easter Island. We may never know what it was.

Probably the most impressive part of the ruins is the section often identified as a fortress because of its high walls, but in fact it's a royal necropolis: Nan Dowas. Some blocks there are an astonishing 5 m long (15 ft.) and one, in one of the corners, is the size of a large truck. As Childress reports, there was a suspicion that it was natural rock, already in place as part of the rock base (which is actually in the ocean, on a coral reef), but excavations have revealed that it was indeed placed there with all the other basalt columns.

Nan Madol sits on a coral reef of limestone, which has been produced by coral activity on the southeast coast of the island. In other words, there is no such basalt floor. Childress describes also a curious incident in which the compass needle "danced" freely, spinning all around its axis, but it might have been actually something natural: volcanic, crystallized basalt is usually magnetized. It's true, however, as he himself remarked, that the needle should not rotate chaotically like he saw.

Another strange fact reflecting the unusual character of this city is the existence of numerous tunnels connecting various islets or specific, important buildings. Probably most of them are presently flooded, used only by sea fish, but the question they raise remains unanswered. Certain tunnels lead into the sea, pointing to the other islands. Why were they built at all? What was the purpose of the city in general? None of the islets resemble a residential district (unlike in Mohenjo Daro for example).

One of the greatest challenges is posed by the existence of the part of the city which lies underwater. It's hardly visible from the shore, usually only the largest blocks or lines of columns are recognizable. Even these can sometimes be seen only by divers or from the air, because of the constant build-up of material by the coral reef. But there can be no doubt that its existence is a fact. Hambruch was the first to map the underwater ruins; perhaps 100 years ago the traces were slightly better visible. It seems likely that the flooded part is comparable in size with the ruins on the surface, i.e., might have occupied an area on the order of ten square miles, which would make this place a true metropolis of the ancient world—literally of the antediluvian world in this case! Apart from that there are traditions saying that a second, separate city is hidden under the waves nearby—the city of the gods that was never found! It's known as "Kahnihmweiso."

A certain light was shed on these mysteries at the end of the 1970s, when the local authorities decided to create an archaeological national park. Before starting any work however, they had to know the extent of the ruins; therefore, a research project was initiated, funded by the United States Government and the Federated States of Micronesia. The Ponape District Historic Preservation Committee hired an American scholar to coordinate the work: Dr. Arthur Saxe from Ohio State University. It was supposed to be the first fully professional, modern research project carried out in Nan Madol. The hopes pinned on it were accordingly very great.

Saxe ascertained, among other things, that the size of the complex mentioned by the previous researchers was accurate (28 km^2), while the "downtown" occupies around 2 km^2. He confirmed the existence of the numerous tunnels as well. The most interesting data were provided however, as could be expected, from the research carried out underwater. In his summary published in 1980 he confirmed, beyond any doubt, that the submerged part exists and that it spans a considerable area. Stone blocks and vertical

159

pillars were situated as deep as 95 feet (29 m) and they formed straight lines leading to the other islands in that area! It was clearly visible on detailed aerial photographs. It involved not just one or two islands, but a significant part of the entire archipelago. What an undertaking!

According to Childress, certain underwater blocks and especially pillars have some signs engraved upon them. They resembled the signs of the writing found in New Zealand. As we know from previously quoted information, the Dravidian (Protodravidian) writing was known in New Zealand, only this fact was forgotten in the 20th century. There were also symmetrical crosses, which we also know as religious symbols. They all occurred in the area in which, according to Hambruch, lay the ruins of the mysterious Kahnihmweiso.

As Childress writes, apart from the official research, there were also certain TV teams which attempted to investigate Nan Madol's secrets. Probably the most interesting and valuable material was filmed by Australian TV, showing among other things the underwater ruins. It is titled "Ponape—the Island of Mystery" and there is a copy of it in the archives of the local college, in the island's capital, Kolonia. Paradoxically it was broadcast only once and passed almost unnoticed.

At the end of this section devoted to Nan Madol it is worth noting certain historical information. The first European to reach Pohnpei was Ferdinand Magellan, in 1595. He noted then that the city was already in ruins and that the inhabitants knew no pottery at all. One can guess therefore, on this basis, that the present peoples of Micronesia peopled these islands long after the builders of Nan Madol left; in any case, there was no contact between them and the latter wave of migration, because fragments of some old pottery were found in the ruins.

In summary, there can be no doubt that Nan Madol is the best evidence for the existence of an extinct civilization which apparently existed in the Pacific before the influx of the cultures that we know today. The "underwater continuation" of the ruins is a phenomenon seen in the case of various other islands, not just in Micronesia. It seems logical that the sunken ruins hide the oldest traces of human occupation. Many such traces of human

160

activity underwater were presented by Graham Hancock in his book *Underworld*. Probably the most convincing is the one called "Yonaguni" off the coast of Japan, which seems to be huge, manmade, and carved out of the matrix rock. Of course, we have to wait for more detailed research which may or may not confirm that it's of artificial origin.

Other information worth noting in this context is the alleged existence of some mysterious writing, the traces of which were supposedly found in Nan Madol. John MacMillan Brown writes in the book mentioned earlier that he discovered the remains of some ancient, dying writing on one of the neighboring islands, or atolls to be exact, named Oleai. It was used only by the chief of the local tribe and, in 1913, only he and four other people were able to read it. Brown claims that the signs did not resemble any other writing he knew.

Anyway, we deal with a curious phenomenon: there is a clear chain of traces across the Indian and Pacific oceans. It's marked not only by the ruins and remnants of certain constructions on the ocean's floor, but also by characteristic writing. One of the most unusual details is, however, that the creators of these traces were ethnically completely different from peoples who arrived there after them. They were obviously tall, but, strangely enough, they had much longer ears than normal people. Let me repeat: the "long eared" apparently occurred in various places along this chain, from India, through the Maldives, on Easter Island and eventually in the South American Andes. That's something that cannot be ignored easily. Another characteristic feature is that they resembled Europeans, among other things having white skin.

The same theme repeats itself in South America. The first Spanish chroniclers often described the Inca rulers as "long eared."[14] There is also no shortage of accounts in which they are characterized as white, even whiter than the Spaniards. For example, Pedro Pizarro, cousin of the conqueror of Peru, wrote in his *Relacion de descubrimiento y conquista del Peru (Regarding the discovery and Conquest of Peru)*:

The daughters of this land's rulers, called Coyas, seem to be women of dignity, and are clean and well-groomed...They consider themselves beautiful and are beautiful indeed. This people have a golden complexion. Among the *rulers* and their women, some have *brighter skin than the Spaniards*. I saw in this country a woman with a child, so bright-skinned, as one can rarely see.

In *La Cronica del Peru (The Chronicles of Peru)*, by Pedro de Cieza de Leon, *in the description referring to Tiahuanaco*, the following fragment can be found: "When we asked the Indians who built these ancient monuments, they replied that it was done by *bearded, white* people, just like us [the Spaniards]."

In order to remove any shadow of a doubt that it was they who reached the Andes through the Pacific, allow me to quote another fragment from one of Kondratov's books—a very important one!—referring this time to a group of islands lying off the coast of Chile. They are situated at a similar latitude to Easter Island, at a similar latitude, only that much closer to the South American coast:

Close to Chile's shore lies the famous "Robinson's Island," that Juan Fernandez named so to honour the Spanish sailor bearing this name, who had discovered it in 1572. After six years his ship was again cutting waves of the south-eastern part of the Great Ocean. A sudden storm drove the ship far south and unexpectedly Juan Fernandez discovered a land hitherto unkown. It's true that the Spanish voyager didn't venture to come to the shore—he only noted that the land is irrigated "by great rivers" and was inhabited by "*white* people, well dressed and in every respect *differing* from the inhabitants of Chile and Peru."[3]

We know already that they represented a people akin to Protodravidians, which also manifested itself in Asia in the form of the Ainuidal migrations such as the Jomon, but their Pacific track forces us to make a clear connection with the populations of

162

the Pacific. Although they resemble mostly the Polynesians, they certainly were not them and it's worth a moment to take a closer look at this problem. One fact has to be realized: at the time in question Polynesia was something altogether different from what it is today. The Polynesians were not a people with the same, molded features, as we know them today.

The racial characteristics of the present population is a result of many migrations, going on over millennia—of constant mixing in other words. There can be no doubt that the first wave differed from the present Polynesians, as well as from present American Indians. One of the most prominent researchers of the oldest Pacific cultures, the New Zealander Peter H. Buck (known also under his Maori name Te Rangi Hiroa) has written a book dedicated specifically to this question, *Vikings of the Pacific*. He wrote:

> As a result of studies over the living people from all the parts of Polynesia it has turned out that the master sailors of the Pacific must be *Europoids*, for they are not characterized by woolly hair, black skin and thin shins of the Negroids, nor by flat face, low height and falling internal epicanthic fold of the Mongoloids. As in the case of other Europoids, also among the Polynesians there is a great variety of the head's shapes. Shapiro has emphasized the worth noticing homogeneousness of certain features, manifesting itself in relatively narrow and high forehead and wide face. It can be stated that there is a domination of short heads in Central Polynesia, in Hawaii and to some degree in the Samoa and Tonga islands. Especially *long heads* occur in New Zealand. This feature is changing in the Mangai as well as in the atolls of Manihiki and Rakahanga within the Cook Islands, to re-emerge on the Marquesas, in the eastern part of the Tuamotu arcipelago and in the Mangareva island, reaching extreme value far in the east—on the Easter Island...
>
> A. C. Haddon claims that the analysis of mixed

population of Indonesia indicates the existence of numerous long-headed elements on the vast area occupied by the short-headed Mongoloids. The long-headed element represented by the Bataks and Dayaks was conventionally named Indonesian. Those "Indonesians" originate probably from the lower reaches of the Ganges river, from where they departed eastwards, to Indonesia, many centuries after the migration of the aboriginal Australians. The short-headed Mongoloids probably wandered southwards even later and eventually outnumbered the Indonesians. As a result of mixing the long-headed Indonesians with short-headed Mongoloids, the Protopolynesians have probably originated— i.e. ancestors of the Pacific sailors. [6]

So, Buck agrees that the ancestors of today's Polynesians (not the modern Polynesians themselves!) represented the Europoidal type, or the white race, and that they originated from the present India and have particularly marked their presence "far in the east—on Easter Island." It's worth remembering! The author of the footnotes to the Polish edition of this book, Professor Aleksander Posern-Zielinski has supplemented it with certain information from "our" field:

Studies of the racial structure of the Polynesians were also carried out by a Polish anthropologist, A. L. Godlewski (1905—1975), who has confirmed the complex anthropological line-up of the eastern Pacific population, being the result of cross-breeding of the black, yellow and white variations. He has also sectioned the so-called pre-Polynesian line-up, being the trace of the Polynesians's *oldest expansion,* characterized by a *decided dominance* of the Europoidal elements over the Mongoloidal and Negroidal, therefore *differing significantly from the later wave* of migration, in which the dominance of yellow variation's racial features was clear.

164

I emphasize one thing once again: the people in question shared certain roots and anthropological features with the later Europeans, but they were not them! These were two (almost) independent branches, with the latter manifesting its activity mostly in the East.

I realize that stating that the colonization of the Americas was carried out by a white people travelling across the Pacific may seem at the very least strange, but that's just what the facts say. Contrary to apperances, New World scholars have had quite a lot to say about it, even apart from the cases like the Kennewick Man, Spirit Cave Mummy and the Ainuidal track that has been found in Ecuador (i.e., the Jomon).

Certain data had already emerged from South America in the 60s and 70s, even before DNA sequencing was available. Scientists decided to carry out blood analysis on the basis of the proteins exctracted from very old Incan mummies, probably representing the ancient aristocracy. It turned out, among other things, that all the mummies had the blood type "A." It had been prevously thought that the blood type was brought to the Americas much later, by the Europeans! It also turned out that all of the blood was devoid of the Rh factor, which occurs on a global scale in only approximately 15% of people. The Spanish *conquistadores* often expressed amazement when they saw members of the Inca ruling layer—a narrow group of people often having whiter skin than the Spaniards themselves. If we could trace back such connections in detail, we would learn that there thrived whole *tribes* of white Indians. In the vicinity of the Peruvian cities of Chimbote and Trujillo, archaeologists unearthed ceramic vases portraying battles waged with some white-skinned warriors. Similar scenes have been depicted in the Temple of the Warriors in the Mayan city of Chichen Itza. Portrayals of bearded figures of various kinds (Amerindians representing the yellow race have essentially no facial hair) with European-like facial features are quite abundant both in Peru, and Mexico. A lot of such "faces" are presented in this book, photographed in public museums—and I didn't have to especially search them out. There are (in Lima, Peru's capital) also mummies described as having blond hair and white skin.

165

Even today finding such Indians is not as unusual as it may seem at first glance. The problem is that so few people realize this in the multi-ethnic societies of South America.

When I was in Chile, I had the opportunity to learn that there is a native group preserving significant independence and cohesion— the Mapuche Indians. Neither the Incas nor the Spaniards had managed to subordinate them and effectively incorporate them into their state organisms. They live in the south of the country, in the present "Araucania" and "Los Lagos" regions, and to a lesser extent in the neighboring part of Argentina. It's roughly the same area in which Monte Verde is located, and that's precisely the "point of arrival" suggested by the sea currents flowing across the Southern Pacific. According to a census, there are several hundred thousand of them. They—as a tribe—are not white skinned (although their skin is much brighter than that of the better known Indians), but certainly they have facial features very far from Mongoloidal. In this respect they are the best evidence for the tremendous variety of the South American Indians, much greater than in North America. Some Mapuches, however, would be hard to recognize as such were they to be moved, experimentally, to the downtown of some European city.

They are not the only representatives of native populations displaying clear Europoidal features; there is also a group in Argentina. Presently it's the "most white" country on this continent, but not because there were no Indians; there were many, only they were subjected to a kind of "mini-Holocaust" in the 19th century, a planned policy of extermination which led to the elimination of at least 40,000 people. The Argentine equivalent of the Mapuches was the Tehuelche tribe, or nation. They were even more interesting as a trace of the described oceanic migration. After the "mini-Holocaust" some of them survived in the mountains, in the west. In the provincial capital, San Carlos de Bariloche (or just Bariloche), there is the Museo de Patagonia, with a certain part of the exhibition dedicated to them. One of the most striking items is the bust portraying the Tehuelche chief (or king if you like). I have to admit that when I saw it, I thought that it was some east-European colonizer, until I saw the description. He looks just like the first Polish king whose visage decorates one of our bank notes. The Tehuelche chief clearly has (or had) a long, tall skull; an aquiline, elongated nose; a barely marked so-called epicanthic fold (eyebrow fold, contrary to Mongoloids); and a *moustache*, and I mean *handlebars*. He resembles a European medieval warrior or peasant, rather than one of his supposed colleagues who arrived through the Bering land bridge from eastern Siberia. A photograph of this bust is reproduced in this book, so you may check out whether my description is accurate.

But, as in the case of the white Incas, he represented the narrow ruling layer. A couple of years earlier I had an experience which I now realize proves that the white ruling caste scheme can be applied to the Chilean Mapuches as well. I was there as a tourist, wanting to see the magic landscape of what's called in Europe the "Chilean Switzerland," decorated by majestic, always snow-capped volcanos. One of them lies just in the heart of the Mapuche land, in the lake district, and is called Villarrica. When I was there, I heard that one of the things worth seeing were the caves on the slopes of the volcano, quite high, which were carved by a kind of underground river of molten lava. I had never seen anything like this, so I decided to get there, somehow, although I had no car and it was too far to walk (the entire cone measures over 20 km in diameter). I decided to try hitchhiking, knowing that the people there are hospitable and helpful. I didn't have to wait long. A young couple from Santiago in a Toyota picked me up. I took my place in the back seat, along side their 6 year-old daughter. Her mother was sitting in front of me and I could only marvel at her long blond hair. The daughter constantly bombarded me with questions and so a certain conversation was maintained. At some point I asked them what the purpose of their trip was; I was just curious if the Chileans themselves were coming as tourists to this area; did they realize and appreciate that they have such beautiful places? I will never forget the daughter's reply: "*Mi mama es Mapuche*," (My mother is Mapuche). They went on to say that they came to visit her family, but also that she is some important figure in their tribal hierarchy and had arrived to take part in some ceremony. I was literally left speechless, for she looked like a Swede, especially with her blue eyes. To be honest, I would never believe that something like this was possible, had I not seen it with

167

my own eyes.

This strange picture has been supplemented in recent years by the results of genetic studies. Among other things, these enabled scientists to establish the approximate age of the Indian population, in other words, to say when the migration(s) took place. Results were published in the magazine *Archaeology* and suggested that the oldest migration or migrations were no later than approximately 21,000 years ago, and more likely around 30,000 years ago. This indicated that they probably didn't come through Beringia, for it only started to emerge as late as 25,000 years ago. Another significant discovery determined that:

> Polynesians and Amerinds*** do share some genetic material. This can be explained either as the retention of ancestral Asian sequences in both populations or by a mixing, either ancient or recent, of the two populations. In 1994 Cann argued that a Polynesian genetic contribution to Amerinds could account for the presence of mtDNA† lineage B in both populations. According to a 1993 study, the lineage *is more common in South American Indians,* becomes less common as one goes north and is rare or absent in NaDene and Eskimo-Aleuts†† If it is an ancestral lineage that came across the Bering land bridge, why is it absent in the north, but present in South America?
>
> The distribution, Cann believes, may better fit a Polynesian origin of the B lineage in Amerinds. In 1995 Bryan Sykes of the Institute of Molecular Medicine at the University of Oxford found that two Polynesian mtDNA sequences, unrelated to the B lineage, matched Amerind sequences. These, he said, could be evidence of contact.
>
> Bonatto and his colleagues attempted to compare all available mtDNA data from Pacific, Amerind and Siberian populations in order to test the possibility of Polynesian-Amerind contacts. They found one more sequence shared between

Polynesians and Amerinds in addition to the two described by Sykes. But when they arranged the mtDNA sequences in a branching tree-shaped diagram according to their similarities, all three cases appeared in low positions from which both Asian and Amerind sequences originate. According to Bonatto, this indicates that the shared sequences are better explained as a retention of ancestral Asian sequences by both Polynesians and Amerinds rather than as the result of later mixing of the populations.††† Bonatto calculated that the B lineage of Polynesians and Amerinds diverged ca. 30,000 years ago, more than 28,000 years before the arrival of Polynesians on Easter Island. [24]

One may, of course, consider it as evidence that apart from the migration through Alaska, there was also another, independent path straight to South America across the Pacific, which could account for all the differences between North American and South American Indians. It also casts doubt on the presently known, late date of the peopling of Easter Island, for if the migration took place so early ("ca. 30,000 years ago"), it probably would have left some traces on this, and other islands, only they have not been discovered yet.

Polynesians were famous for their ability to cover large distances at sea. Their equipment has not changed for centuries and we may risk an assumption that at the time of the eastward migration it was quite similar to that known from the first historical relations. They built ships of various kinds, depending on the distance and the number of people they were supposed to carry.

One model dominated however. It had a wooden hull made of planks, tied to each other with ropes twined through small holes made on the edges. Connections were sealed with special resins. At the hull's center stood the mast (in some instances there were two or three masts), holding the sail woven mostly from the leaves of the pandana tree. Additional propulsion, just as in the case of Vikings ships, was provided by paddles. They were, however, short, not fixed in rowlocks, and the crew paddled facing the boat's bow, like in kayaks of the American Indians. Some ships were equipped with stabilizing floats installed on booms, which enabled large decks to be constructed on them, so the boats weren't necessarily crowded. Larger types had something resembling roofed compartments for the crew. For exploration treks usually the largest models were built, with two hulls connected by wide decks. Their length was in the 20m range (66 ft.), but some as long as 30m long were seen. Some could carry as many as 100 or more passengers, including women and children. As provisions, the Polynesian sailors took, among other things, dried sweet potatos, cooked fruits, dried fish, special mussels that could be dried, as well as certain live animals such as poultry, fed with dried coconut pulp, various grains and so on. In a central part of the deck there was a place prepared for a fireplace, where, on a layer of sand, the food could be prepared, and a chicken (or a shark caught along the way) could be baked. Fresh water was carried in hollowed gourds, coconut shells and even in the bamboo rods that were a part of the ship's construction! It is estimated that in this way they could travel for 3-4 weeks, eating modestly, but without starving. That's quite a while. Huge distances such as those from Easter Island to the Chilean coast (approx. 3200 km) or from the Tuamotu archipelago to Easter Island (approx. 2000 km) could be covered quite normally. From the technical point of view it was possible.[6]

If the anthropological/genetic similarities could be seen to testify to the existence of the "Axis," then establishing the chain of traces marking the migration wouldn't still be such a serious challenge. It wouldn't necessarily prove that a transfer of culture and civilization was taking place. Of course the primary evidence for such a maturity of this heritage poses already the very existence of the "Axis," the geographic coordination of the three points: Mohenjo Daro—Nan Madol—Easter Island. It's indisputible that there was sophisticated knowledge involved; probably both as a "tool" enabling the whole undertaking, and as the "medium" that was transferred to the new continent to make the development possible, i.e., it did not develop from scratch. The same elements occur along the entire track—the writing, the cult of the "bird-men," religion, the social system with the "long eared"—from the Maldives all the way up to the Incas, and so on.

This also clearly suggests that the people weren't on a blind quest in search for something, but a pre-planned undertaking carried out by a civilization. Contacts were not being made by some isolated groups of prospectors, as scholars *can* see it.

There is one very strong element confirming that South America was the scene of an outburst of high civilization in the remote past, only it was later forgotten, or even the material remains were deliberately destroyed. It is the writing—many kinds of it, to be precise—which serves as an example of how different the truth really is from the official version, if only one takes a closer look. It's strange that it is ignored, when one takes into account the huge number of scientific publications on this subject (which are ignored too!).[25,26,27,28,29,30,31] I will cite only a few, selected examples.

The "bustrophedonic" writing known from Easter Island did have its Andean continuation, but what's more interesting, is that it was by no means the only kind of writing that was used by the Incas, or by the other Andean cultures before them. This question was studied by numerous researchers from South America itself and from Europe mostly before World War Two and shortly thereafter, but found virtually no reflection in the works of their North American counterparts in the main academic centers afterwards. The notion that the Incas never knew any system of writing is a myth lacking any grounds, just like the view that they didn't know the wheel. I personally saw a toy in the Rafael Larco Herrera Museum in Lima which was equipped with wheels. There is an interesting analogy in this respect with the Japanese civilization, which never used vehicles on wheels, although the idea as such was pretty well known,—but that's just a digression.

The research pertaining to the South American system of writing didn't penetrate the North American academic barrier, despite tremendous effort, and adequate results, on the part of the South American scientists. One of them had outstanding merits in this field, although he was and still is hardly known outside this continent. He is the Argentine Dick Edgar Ibarra-Grasso (1914—2000) who lived in Bolivia for 23 years, until 1940, and this was the period when he gathered most of the data. Writing was probably his main area of interest and he managed to prove that the Indians used not just one, but four different kinds of writing. In

1967 his main, monumental work was published in Buenos Aires which is still, in my opinion, one of the best publications devoted to the prehistory of this continent.[32] There is a whole chapter describing the various systems of writing, with lots of references and reproductions of specific examples. I believe that most of it is unknown to North American archaeologists in general.

Ibarra-Grasso was a layman, although his methods and the effects of his work were professional in the full sense of the word. This was reflected by the exceptional esteem he enjoyed in Bolivia. He discovered and unearthed, among other things, the ruins of eight ancient temples. He was also a founder of a regional museum in Sucre, partime capital of Bolivia, and has written, obviously, countless scientific publications on these topics. He died in Buenos Aires, essentially a forgotten man. We will return to his legacy, but as a kind of introduction to this issue I would like to quote again a fragment from one of Kondratov's books:

> Excavations from the territory of Peru, Bolivia, Ecuador and Chile have unearthed hundreds of archaeological cultures, scientists say. The time-frame of their occurence, the degree of spreading, their mutual interactions, sometimes even the chronology of their birth—these are all problems concerning South American archaeology worked out even to a lesser degree than similar subjects referring to Central America. Very often even a single finding shatters the existing scheme. That's why many theses remain contentious even today and South America's modern history—murky. The best way of penetrating the mysteries of extinct civilizations is by making oneself acquainted with the written sources left after them. But the writing of South America fell victim to an unusual twist of fate. We will tell about it in detail, because the history of the Andean hieroglyphs illustrates, undoubtedly in the best way, the riddles of the New World's oldest civilizations—in the area where to this day the most amazing discoveries are

possible.

"In the old times," writes one of the chroniclers from the 15th century, „the supreme ruler of the Incas gathered in his capital, Cuzco, the wisemen from all the provinces subordinated to him and asked them about the most important events from bygone times. Later on he ordered the history of each ruler to be described, as well as the history of the lands which they had conquered. Also the traditions on the origin of the Incas were described, the legend of the deluge and a number of other tales and myths. These texts had been immortalized on great sheets, glued onto large boards and set in frames of pure gold. The tables were stored in a special compartment in the "Temple of the Sun." Entrance was accessible only for the supreme ruler of the Incas and for specific scholars (amautas), who were able to read and interprete the texts."

There comes a time, however, that Cuzco along with the "Temple of the Sun" is conquered by Pizzarro's band. Great was the Spaniards's awe at the sight of the great canvases portraying the Inca rulers affixed with mysterious inscriptions. The conquerors were not interested in the inscriptions (their commander, Francisco Pizzarro, never learned to write even in Spanish). It wasn't the canvases' content that attracted their attention, but their frames—gold! And the priceless works of Inca writing shared the sad fate of other Inca treasures. The frames were melted down and the canvases were disposed of "as useless."

It's worth adding that this sad fate met not all the canvases: four were sent as a gift for the Spanish king—Felipe II. It was in 1572. Since then, however, there is no trace of them. They didn't get to Spain nor were they returned to Peru. Did the ship sink, or did something else happen? There is no answer to this question. Most likely the canvases rest on the ocean's floor, sunk along with the crew and the cargo by an English corsair.

The loss is all the more bitter for science in that no traces of Inca writing are preserved in Peru. And not just because they were framed in gold. The Incas themselves should be blamed in this instance, for it was they who "took care" that no written document remained in their empire, with the exception of the canvas kept in the "Temple of the Sun." Legend has it that during the rule of one of the kings an epidemic broke out. In spite of the priests's prayers, the epidemic was raging. Then the Inca asked the oracle of the supreme god, Viracocha, a question: "how to put an end to the plague?" The oracle supposedly answered that "using writing should be forbidden." The Inca ruler and the highest priest at the same time listened to the oracle and forbade the use of writing in his land. And when a scholar priest—amauta—didn't obey the order he was burned alive, as a warning for other heretics. [2]

According to Ibarra-Grasso it was Pachacutec VII who forbade the use of writing.

The phrase "Andean system of writing" is usually associated with "quipu," the Inca knot writing. It was thought until recently that only numbers were recorded in this way. One of the archaeological breakthroughs of the century was, however, the discovery of a sample representing a derivative (being a kind of hybrid) with hieroglyphs: the knots were replaced by complex, multi-colored elements. It was a derivative of the "basic" system. The discovery was all the more significant in that the sample was supplemented with a thorough linguistic description from the epoch! It was discovered in one of the private libraries in Italy in the mid-1990s. It turned out that, impelled by the influence of various uncanny tales and rumors arriving from South America at the beginning of the 17th century, two Italian monks decided to go to Peru, on their own, apparently precisely in order to gather information "at the source" about the intriguing, local system of writing. As a result, a thorough treatise was produced. Its authors were in a unique position, since the beginning of the 17th century was a period when, in certain isolated enclaves such as Machu Picchu, there still existed survivors of the former educated caste who possessed the knowledge of it, i.e., the aristocracy, priests, and so on. The treatise' authors presented in their notebooks (which became densely written booklets) several signs of writing in color and even attached a sample of the original. It was a fragment of a quipu string, not with simple knots however, but containing certain symbols woven from multi-colored wool. Even though similar symbols were occasionally found much earlier, there is a difference between single signs detached from the context, and a comprehensive treatise on the subject. This whole story was described in an issue of *Archaeology* magazine from 1996, and I will quote the most interesting fragments of the article and of the original Italian manuscript that has been extensively cited in it (emphasis again by me):

> An Inka accounting system that used knotted strings called quipus to record numerical data has long been known to scholars. The complexity and number of knots indicated the contents of warehouses, the number of taxpayers in a given province, and census figures. Were quipus also used to record calendars, astronomical observations, accounts of battles and dynastic successions, and literature? If so, all knowledge of such use has been lost—or has it? At a conference of Andean scholars this past June, Laura Laurencich Minelli, a professor of Precolumbian studies at the University of Bologna, described what she believes to be a seventeenth-century Jesuit manuscript that contains detailed information on literary quipus. According to the document:
>
> Quechua... is a language similar to music and has several keys: a language for everyone; a holy language, [which] was handed [down]

only by knots; [and] another language [that] was handed [down] by means of woven textiles and by pictures on monuments and in jewels and small objects. I will tell you… about the quipu, which is a complicated device composed of colored knots… There is a general quipu used by everyone for numbering and daily communication and another quipu for keeping all religious and caste secrets, known only to the Kings, the Virgins of the Sun, the Priests and the Philosophers. [Many of] these latter quipus, which could easily be read by [Father Blas] Valera, were destroyed by the Spaniards. The Inka authorities collected the most significant of them and locked them up in arks of unripe gold… in order to avoid falling into the hands of Catholic priests. A monolith was fastened to the arks as ballast, and they were plunged into Lake Titicaca and hidden in the Orcos Valley."

Surfacing at a time when decipherment of these string documents is at a standstill, the manuscript, if authentic, could be a Rosetta stone for Andean scholarship….

An explanation of the Quechua language follows, including a grammar and two Inka prayers. The most complete description of the literary quipu is in this part of the text:

"I visited… archives for those quipus that tell the true story of the Inka people and that are hidden from commoners. These quipus differ from those used for calculations as they have elaborate symbols… which hang down from the main string… These royal quipus do not exist anymore; they were burned by the Spaniards out of ignorance, and by many priests…

The scarceness of the words and the possibility of changing the same term using particles and suffixes to obtain different meanings allow them to realize a spelling book with neither paper, nor ink, nor pens… [The] curaca emphasized that this quipu is based by its nature on the scarceness of words, and its composition key and its reading key lie in its syllabic division… [The] curaca explained: 'if you divide the word Pachacamac [the Inka deity of earth and time] into syllables Pa-cha-ca-mac, you have four syllables. If you… want to indicate the word 'time'—'pacha' in Quechua, it will be necessary to make two symbols [in the quipu] representing Pachacamac—one of them with a little knot to indicate the first syllable, the other with two knots to indicate the second syllable'… [The curaca] listed the main key words with an explanation of how to realize them in quipus."

…Oliva [one of the monks] gives definitions for symbols known as *tocapu*, that appear in many Inka weavings. There is also a strange diagram of black and white lines and balls, which Oliva labels the "Quipu of Acatanga." Beside it are detailed instructions for reading it:

"Quipucamayoc Chauarurac reconstructed on paper, with the skill of his colonized hands, the… quipu that I discovered incomplete in… Atacanga's huaca [shrine] in [Bolivia in] 1627. He himself specified that this quipu was woven by some huacacamayoc [shrine keeper] using a little loom in the years before Pizarro's arrival. Because of its roughness and for being a relic of its people, it was very difficult to find a quipu like this, containing Sumac Nusta's song. When I saw Chahuarurac's uncertain drawings, I remembered others that Valera… had given me."

According to Oliva, stanzas from the Inka poem "Sumac Nusta" (Beautiful Princess) were recorded both on a wool quipu fragment he found in Bolivia and in the drawings given him by Valera, both of which are enclosed in the manuscript….

Ruiz was entrusted with recopying Valera's

text and drawings. Valera returned to Spain, where he died in 1619. Oliva says that he was buried in the town of Alcala de Henares near Madrid, along with a quipu on which he knotted "the story of the Inkas."...

Naples, 1985: Clara Miccinelli, Carlo Miccinelli's cousin, is working in the family archive when she comes across the manuscript and the quipu fragment. After four years of research with fellow historian Carlo Animato, Miccinelli publishes her findings in a small volume "Quipu: The Talking Knots of the Mysterious Inka" (1989), which receives little attention from the academic community...

Clearly *most* of the historical information contained in the manuscript is in conflict with our current understanding of the Spanish conquest of Peru, which is based on the writings of Garcilaso de la Vega, the Spanish Jesuit Bernabe Cobo, Guaman Poma de Ayala and numerous official communications between Spain and its New World colony. [47]

Quipu is, contrary to the official position, one of the significant proofs that there existed a transfer of culture from Asia, for an *identical system of writing* was discovered in Korea, on the other side of the great ocean.[33]

According to the description quoted above and other sources, the aforementioned "literary" quipu was created by combining the normal knots with a certain system of signs known as "tocapu." Although the holy records "destroyed and hidden in the Orcos Valley" were lost, the signs of tocapu (as a separate system) have been well known for decades, only they were usually considered merely ornaments on textiles—they occur mostly in this form.

Tocapu existed in two variations—one of them occurred in the form of rectangular or squared signs ("tocapu proper") and the other in the form of ovals. Both of them shared a certain unique feature: they were complex and colorful. One has the impression

An old print of the Gate of the Sun at Tiahuanaco, Bolivia.

that even slight changes in the colors—various shades—mattered. In this respect, as hieroglyphs, they are certainly unique and even quite peculiar. Both are presented in the illustrations; please note that specific signs were repeated very rarely, which suggests that there must have been a large number of them. One of the enclosed representations of tocapu ends up with a swastika. Perhaps it's just a coincidence, but in one of the earlier chapters there is a reproduction of some writing discovered in New Zealand, which also ends up with a swastika, although it resembles rather the Easter Island writing. It's one more confirmation that a lot of elements in the Andean cultures in fact originate from the other side of the Pacific.

It seems that both versions of tocapu were "recorded" not only on textiles, but in the "literary quipu" as well. The samples enclosed in and described by the Italian manuscript are rectangular, but in the museums of Lima I saw numerous examples of quipu with colorful elements resembling the oval variation, which was called "signos pallar." Both are quite similar, but one cannot rule out the possibility that they in fact represented two different systems of writing.

Recently I found a very interesting publication on this topic, published in Poland in 1974, written by a scientist. It's an analysis of this phenomenon, containing a lot of unknown facts, so I will again translate certain fragments:

> Until recently the "Peruvian writing" was identified only and solely with quipu, despite the fact that for at least 7 years extremely interesting research by a Peruvian scholar Victoria de la Jara has been known, who proved that at least three kinds of writing were known in precolombian Peru....
>
> First and foremost, even before the Spaniards's arrival there existed in the quechua language a clear distinction between the spoken language, "runa simi" and the written language, "simi qillca." Analysis of the "qillca" word (to write, draw or writing, drawing) and its derivatives has demonstrated the existence of such phrases as "written clothes" and the close connection between expressions "the one who draws and paints signs" and "the one who knows the past."
>
> Secondly, it has to be clearly emhasized that in the 16th-17th centuries only alphabetical recording was considered writing in the strict sense of this word, all other kinds (even Chinese writing, well known to Europeans) were "just pictures and drawings" (Jose de Acosta, around 1590). The same Acosta states clearly that "[Indians from Peru] compensated the lack of writing with paintings and drawings on boards." He adds that the great ruler of the Incas, Inca Pachacuti, ordered the entire history of his nation to be "painted" on great boards, which were then stored in the Puqin-Kancha temple. Another chronicler, Miguel Caballo Balboa recalls that Inca Wayna Kapac "feeling near death, made a testament according to an old custom, that is, he

marked multi-colored strokes on a great stick, so that his last will was known."

Of course, accounts of this kind, as well as all chronicle records, should be approached with due caution, however, summarizing the etymological and source research, the existence of a graphic system of recording in precolombian Peru may be considered proven.

Victoria de la Jara's main merit was pointing attention to the fact that signs viewed hitherto as ornaments may be writing. Respective statistical studies confirmed her assumptions. It has turned out by this method that the origins of Peruvian writing date back to the 3rd century B.C. The oldest traces of writing come from the Paracas-Necropolis culture (southern coast of Peru), which are the so-called signos-pallar, or bean signs, occurring on funeral textiles, the so-called fardos. Signos-pallar were found on 41 textiles originating from 13 various fardos ("fardo," the name of mummy's "wrapping," consisting of several layers of textiles).

Ms. de la Jara has classified 325, mostly two-colored signs. They occur usually in pairs, according to the principle of simple formal oppositions. Signs of a numerical record were deciphered and based on the bi-decimal system.$^{\infty}$ Similar signs were discovered on Nazca culture's textiles, from 8th century A.D. (southern coast of Peru). They probably have been adopted from the Paracas culture. It is also assumed that both cultures were based on a common linguistic foundation. Signos-pallar emerges also in the Mochica culture (northern coast of Peru), albeit their drawings differ from the Paracas and Nazca scheme. This difference becomes clearly visible in the Mochica-B phase (around 800 A.D.) when signs inscribed within circles start to appear, which is interpreted by Victoria de la Jara as a numerical record.

181

In the later period, including the so-called Tiahuanaco horizon, the writing, at least in this form, is vanishing, to be re-born as tocapus in the period of Inca domination.∞ The more surprising is a discovery of signos–pallar, painted on a wall of a 17th century church, on the northern coast of Peru.

The researcher dealt mostly with the aforementioned tocapu signs, which constitute in her view the second Inca "writing" (and third Peruvian, after signos pallar and the "regular" quipu)… One of the first deciphered signs [of tocapu] was the "Sapan Inca" symbol, the ruler's title. The researcher used to this end, among other things, the information given by chroniclers about a similar sign, the so-called "aspe" woven only on the robe of the last independent ruler of the Incas, Atahualpa. Succesively, basing on the Inca number of four ("tawa" in quechua) she has deciphered the signs related to time and space, such as "Pacha," the world, timespace and "Inti," the Sun. She has also determined the function of colors. One of them is the change of the same sign's meaning depending on the colors of the specific parts in the pattern. For example: the "Chaska" sign (Venus) may also be read as "Punchaw," the day, or "tuta," the night, depending on the coloring of the fields in corners. According to the same rule, the "Inti" sign may be used for determining the seasons of the year or the time of day. This function is tied with the general symbolics of colors: brown = dry, blue = water, black = night, as well as three colors attributed to celestial bodies: red = Sun, white = Moon, yellow = stars (ties with the symbolics of colors in quipu are rather loose). To express complex ideas new signs were created, being clusters of two or more other ones, for example: "the eclipse of the Sun" by connecting the "Inti" and "Mama Quilla" signs.

Alternatively, several tocapus were clustered into one word. In this case the grammatical relationships were marked, according to Victoria de la Jara, by subtle alterations of colors in the case of certain parts of a sign (another function of color) or by introducing additional dots or lines. Unfortunately, the researcher does not give clear examples for such a role of colors. I personally managed, on the basis of the modest material at my disposal, to extract two cases in which the role of color corresponds probably with possessives in the third person (singular and plural). Passing on to attempts of deciphering longer "texts," Victoria de la Jara has noticed the influence of figural scenes and symbols accompanying the inscription on the text's meaning. In one group of "keros" it was about changes in the inscription depending on whether the Inca stands or sits, whether a woman standing in front of him gives him a white or red flower, and whether a hummingbird appears by the flower or not. Similarly however, as in the case when colors have a grammatical meaning, the researcher doesn't specify what these changes consist of... It is interesting that despite the fact that most of the keros originate from the colonial period, they are devoid of any Christian symbols... The longest of the so far deciphered texts is the so-called Epitaph of Inca Pachacuti, from a kero of A-3 type, No. 24. The inscription consists of 30 signs, in 3 rows with 10 signs in each, with 12 central signs sectioned off in a symmetrical layout. This layout is also a carrier of information. Thirty tocapus symbolize the 30 day month in the Inca calendar, 12 central ones = 12 months in a year, and the whole–the 360-day Inca year.°°°°°

The text can be read in two ways, according to the researcher:

First two rows:

183

"The grave of the Great Pachacuti from Cuzco. The valiant Pachacuti, great lord of the Cuzco people."

Third row:

"Inti, the luminous, the fertile mother; Inti, the supreme lord. The luminous Moon; Apu, the creator."

De la Jara adds that the form of the developed inscription may symbolize the sign "Hatun," Great. The results of these translations are not complete, however, and in some cases not even particularly convincing. Translations of some inscriptions don't seem to agree with the quechua grammar. The following conclusions arise:

1. As Professor Knorozov [who deciphered the Mayan writing] supposes, the meanings of signs should be specified or changed; it is characteristic that Professor Barthel translates certain signs differently from Victoria de la Jara.

2. Due to the lack of any trace of using verbs, the tocapus should be considered a developed ideographic system rather than writing in the strict sense. It also isn't certain if the symbols should be read in the quechua language and not in *pukina*—which was the language known only to the Inca aristocracy.§

The punchline of this discovery is whereas the fact that it has been accomplished by an amateur, based on materials known to archaeologists and historians for some decades at least. And that's what some scholars cannot forgive Mrs de la Jara.
48

The aforementioned language of the Inca aristocracy deserves certain further explanation. There can be no doubt that it would be a key to their written history, "*would be*," for it is in all probability lost forever. The language would also certainly give us the answer to the all more important question: who were these people? The descendents of sages?

It's hard to find any comprehensive information about it, but I found a few mentions. In a book devoted to the Peruvian cultures, published in 1985, one can find the following passage: "While the quechua and aymara languages are to this day used by millions of Indians, the third of Peru's languages—*pukina*—has disappeared almost without trace."[50]

The American Professor Alan Kolata, author of the only decent monograph on Tiahuanaco (which he spells "Tiwanaku") and Puma Punku (described in the next chapter), has written that the people in question were particularly tied with this crucial place:

> It is likely that at least three of these languages were spoken by the various ethnic groups that were incorporated in the Tiwanaku state: Uru-Chipaya, Puquina [or Pukina] and proto-Aymara. The question of which of these was the dominant language remains unresolved. Arguments based on the distribution of toponyms and other lexical markers have been formulated to demonstrate that *Puquina* was *the original language of the Tiwanaku people* (Torero 1974, Hardman 1979, 1981)...
>
> The Pukina [people], now *extinct*, were distributed along the lake shores and in the sub-tropical valleys of the Andes' eastern slopes and may have been the principal wetland originators of raised field technology. [49]

He has also written that there was a division into two ethnically distinct groups of people—the ruled ones and the rulers—as with Easter Island: "Tiwanaku society and its principle of dual corporate organization might have been generated by the creative encounter and tension filled interaction between mobile herding groups of proto-Aymara origin with sedentary agricultural groups of Pukina origin, with the latter retaining a measure of higher prestige." [49]

Summarizing, we have two peculiar kinds of South American hieroglyphs: the tocapus and signos–pallar, but that's not all. Ibarra–Grasso has described a third kind: the bustrophedonic writing, written alternately from left to right and from right to left, that looks like a modified, simplified version of the Easter Island writing.[29,32] It was found at the turn of the 1940s and 50s in Bolivia, and shortly after that it became the subject of extensive study. Only a couple of examples exist, written on sheepskin. It was found—a characteristic fact—in the vicinity of Tiahuanaco! It was known as "quillca" or "chinchi recado," the latter pertaining to the vestigial form used even long after the conquest of Bolivia and Peru, for a certain local priest has discovered a prayer book written by the local Indians in that language! The word "quillca," as we know from the article cited above, probably just means "writing." E. Nordenskjöld has discovered a similar bustrophedonic writing in Panama as well, containing even the characteristic element of the "bird-men."

There are many more similarities testifying that the "Pacific track" may be substantiated, even in the case of its South American extension. As I mentioned, these originate from fields other than archaeology itself, (such as ethnography, for example), and as such are hardly known to archaeologists:

1. As early as in the first half of the 19th century, the famous German traveller and researcher Alexander von Humboldt, noticed that the Hindu zodiac signs are almost identical with the respective signs of the Maya;[14]

2. The Maya calendar of eclipses was calculated according to exactly the same scheme as the Chinese method from the time of the Han dynasty;[19]

3. The famous and elaborate Inca system of postal messengers (and spies), indispensable in managing such a long (almost 4000 km) and mountainous state, was known on the western side as well, in India. One of the first chroniclers who described it was the 14th century Arab traveler Ibn Batuta. He writes that apart from the regular state postal system (the "berid"), there also existed an "express" mail system known as "ulak," which was *as fast as a falcon and thanks to the perfectly organized*

system of shifts and relays, covered in few days the tremendous distance from the northern mountains to the southern seas."[5] In Tahuantinsuyu, the Inca empire, this system was so effective that if the ruler wished on some day a sea fish for a dinner, it could be delivered fresh. It's worth mentioning that the distance in a straight line between the Pacific coast and Cuzco was on the order of 350km (over 200 miles) and the difference in altitude, 3410 m. (11180 ft.)! The messengers were often changed, to which end special inns were constructed. If it was possible, they shouted messages across a mountain pass, for example, or gave special signs that allowed messages to be passed over without actually traversing the terrain;

4. Just as in the Andes, on many mountainous islands of Polynesia and Micronesia crops were cultivated on raised fields or terraces, up to the very mountain tops. Such terraces still cover around 5% of the Palan island in Micronesia. It is interesting that the present inhabitants of Palan do not know who built these terraces. This method of cultivation is of course used in Asia as well;

5. It is a little known fact that the ritual Maya ball game, "pok-a-tok," was also known in Peru as "tachtli," and in a similar form in ancient India;[5]

6. The problem of similarities between these two areas was dealt with in the 1930s by a Scandinavian ethnologist, Erland Nordenskjöld. He ascertained a whole series of various correlations. Identical were, for example, the weapons used in Polynesia and Peru: blow guns to throw small darts, and flattened, trapesoid shaped clubs studded with sharps stone flakes at the edges (or with obsidian, the volcanic glass). In Peru this weapon, resembling a Roman sword, was made also of bronze, although the obsidian blades were much sharper—a strong warrior could chop off a horse's head;

7. Similar, wide bracelets were worn, and similar toilet utensils were used, such as one which was a hybrid of comb and brush;

8. The same sorts of reed boats were made on Easter Island and the Peruvian coast. They were also used on Lake Titicaca, where they are still in use. They are identical;

9. Identical fishing hooks were known and made in Polynesia and in Peru. The same can be said of ceremonial masks, trumpets made of sea shells and other objects;

10. Quite important and even striking are the similarities relating to the medical arts and the level of their sophistication. The Indians used various anaesthetic substances. Many of the excavated skeletons have tooth fillings, quite similar to modern ones, as well as adhesions after successfull skull trepanations and even fillings in the form of golden plates. It suggests a mastery of brain surgery. Such surgeries weren't carried out anywhere else in the world, except in Polynesia and South America (generally speaking). By the way, these were done on a suspiciously large scale, which suggests that their purpose might not have been solely medical— perhaps they were religious or magical as well;[5]

11. Methods of constructing stone walls and platforms were very similar and unique on the world scale at the same time, which has been described earlier;

12. As could be expected, there are also numerous linguistic analogies. For example, the potato, existing then only in these areas, is known in Polynesia as "kumara," while in Peru it was called "kumar." The *sapindus saponaria* plant, whose juice may be used as a substitute for soap, bears in both areas the same name: "para para." Following the same rule, the gourd is known as "kimi" in both places (an important food for sailors!).

188

First and foremost, however, one has to emphasize the aforementioned similarity of the fundamental religious elements: the same gods occur in Polynesia and in Peru and Bolivia: Tane (pronounced the same in both areas), and Kon Tiki Viracocha in South America vs. Kon Tiki in Polynesia. There is also the unique cult of "bird-men" on Easter Island and in the Andes, plus the "Andean cross" and the Mohenjo Daro cross occurring in identical contexts.

As one more analogy we may consider the occurrence of Europoids, particularly among the aristocracy. The scheme visible in Peru was also apparent throughout Polynesia. Even James Cook was astounded by this; this is how he described his voyage to the Marquesas in 1773: "We have encountered hundreds of truly European faces, and among them—more than one typical Roman nose." Another voyager from the same ship, Johann Forster wrote: "Some of them could be boldly put beside the masterpieces of the ancient art and they surely would not lose anything on this comparison."

One of the local *kings,* named O-Aheatua, was described by Forster in the following way: "He had a brighter skin than all of his lieges and straight, long, light-brown hair, which at the end passed into a reddish-yellow shade."

Forster also mentions a certain peculiar event when one of the Polynesian noblemen, named Porea, was so amazed by his similarity to the visitors that he decided to carry out a certain "experiment," namely, he asked for European dress and the opportunity to join the crew on a planned "tour" of the other islands. Forster provided the following description:

> Dressed in linen jacket and sailor pants, he came ashore with them. He carried a gunpowder horn and Captain Cook's pouch with pellets and asked us to treat him as one of our men. He didn't say anything in his native tongue, only muttered something completely unintelligible, which has indeed confused the local people. In order to make this mystification even easier, he didn't want either to be called his Tahitan name Porea, but asked us to give him some English name.

(Footnotes)

* That is, Hanan and Hurin.

** That is almost 300 pounds.

*** "Amerinds", i.e., American Indians.

† mtDNA, is mitochondrial DNA, genetic material inherited only from mothers, thanks to which it changes slowly, at an almost constant pace and regardless of the rate of cross-breeding .

†† That is, in the far north.

††† Then why they are absent in the northern part of North America?

∞ "Bi-decimal means multiplications of the number 20.

∞∞ So the square signs would be an evolved form of the bean–signs or signos pallar.

∞∞∞ It's striking how similar this calendar was to ours, which in turn was inherited from the Sumerian empire, which based calculations on multiplications of the number 12, hence our day counts 2 times 12 hours, an hour counts 5 times 12 minutes, and so on.

§ It's another very interesting and mysterious thread, namely, that the Inca ruling caste used a different language from the "more Indian" part of their nation; we know only that such a language existed, nothing more, but it clearly suggests – however strange it may seem – that the two groups had slightly different origins. Again, it resembles the peculiar social order from Easter Island.

The Gate of the Sun at Tiahuanaco, Bolivia. The figure in the center is the Viracocha god, standing on a step platform or pyramid. He holds two snakes symbolizing lightning. He is being adored by rows of bird-men (photo: Igor Witkowski).

The Gate of the Sun at Tiahuanaco, Bolivia.

Top: Detail from the Gate of the Sun – an elephant's head? (photo: Igor Witkowski). Bottom: An American elephant's head from the Museo de Oro in Colombia's capital (photo: Igor Witkowski).

Tiahuanaco statue in kneeling (quizuo) position, nearly identical to the kneeling statue found at Easter Island.

Above: A close-up of the head of the Kon Tiki Viracocha statue at Tiahuanaco. Right: A woodcut from the 19th century portraying the no longer extant stele from Copan in Honduras, showing elephants' heads. According to present knowledge elephants died out in America around 10,000 years ago. Below: Close-up of a block at Puma Punku: the three-dimensional connections of perpendicular surfaces could not be done without a rotating tool!

Tiahuanaco head.

6

THE CITY THAT BREAKS ALL THE RULES

At last we have come to the heart of all the South American and Transpacific mysteries: to Tiahuanaco and the nearby ruins known as Puma Punku.

The name Tiahuanaco refers to the ancient architectural complex lying in northwestern Bolivia, on the Andean plateau (altiplano) of Lake Titicaca. It is presently situated at a distance of some 15 km (10 miles) from the lakeshore, at the "extreme" altitude of 3840 m (12,590 ft.). The ruins aroused sensation and amazement on the part of visitors practically since time immemorial, and they still do. Even for the Quechua and Aymara Indians, the inhabitants of Tahuantinsuyu, it served as a symbol of antiquity, linked with some foreign civilization, as mentioned earlier. Here I quote one of the Spanish chroniclers, Pedro de Cieza de Leon (writing in 1553):

> When one considers the work, I cannot understand or fathom what kind of instruments or tools were used to work them, for it is evident that before these huge stones were dressed and brought to perfection, they must have been much larger to have been left as we see them... I would say that I consider this the oldest antiquity in all of Peru. It is believed that before the Incas reigned, long before, certain of these buildings existed, and I have heard Indians say that the Incas built their great edifices of Cuzco along the lines of the walls to be seen in this place. They go even further and say that the first Incas talked of setting up their court and capital here in Tihuanacu... I asked the natives in the presence of Juan Vargas, who holds an

encomienda over them, if these buildings had been built in the time of the Incas, and they laughed at the question, repeating what I have said, that they were built before they reigned… However, they had heard from their forefathers that all that is there appeared overnight. Because of this and because they also say that bearded men were seen on the island of Titicaca and that these people constructed the building of Vinaque, I say that it might have been before the Incas ruled, there were people of parts in these kingdoms, come from no one knows where, who did these things and who—being few and the natives many—perished in the wars. [49]

It probably was not a city in the usual sense, but rather an administrative and religious center of a once powerful empire. It occupies an area of approximately 2 km² (almost a square mile). According to modern radiocarbon datings, the roots of Tiahuanaco itself date back to around 1500 B.C., but the period of greatest sophistication fell in the first five centuries A.D., and it started to lose its significance at the end of the first millenium. The definitive end came only one to two centuries before the brief expansion and bloom of the Inca empire (the bloom lasted only around a century before the Spanish conquest; the Incas are therefore merely the tip of the iceberg in South American history). It wasn't, however, just the city, but an entire state, which at the end of its existence was essentially absorbed by the Incas. One may therefore risk a claim that the Incas, with but few exceptions, were not the creators of most of the achievements for which they are often accredited; they only inherited and transformed the patrimony of much older cultures and civilizations, with Tiahuanaco clearly being the main inspiration and source. The famous intricate road system was in large part built by the Tiahuanaco civilization, for example.

But why is this city or center so important from the point of view of this book? For many reasons, many of which have been mentioned in the previous chapters. Apart from the "links" listed at the end of the previous chapter connecting the Pacific basin with South America in general, there are also elements specific to

Tiahuanaco. Let me summarize them briefly:

1. Very strong religious connections with the same gods: the central place in Tiahuanaco was occupied by the figure portraying Viracocha (known as Kon Tiki Viracocha), who is also present on the famous "Gate of the Sun" at Tiahuanaco. The other god, Tane, also has Polynesian roots. There is also the "copy" of the characteristic figure of a kneeling bearded man (god?), known from Mohenjo Daro and Easter Island. Tiahuanaco is also considered a center of the "bird-men" cult, as evidenced by Heyerdahl in his magnificent book *The Art of Easter Island*, plus it's associated with the "Andean cross," which is visible in many places out there. These elements create a clear link with our Axis. I saw in the local museum very clear portrayals of the Make Make god as well. "Benett's monolith," unearthed in Tiahuanaco, very strongly resembles the figure of a bearded man standing close to the Ahu Vinapu platform, on Easter Island;

2. The city was supposedly raised by some white, red-haired, tall incomers, possessing great knowledge;

3. The art of stonecutting and the construction of the walls and platforms is very similar to that found on the island.

These are by no means all the reasons, the most important part of which are described at the end of this chapter. The greatest thing to bear in mind is that Tiahuanaco was simply the oldest such source of civilization in the entire western hemisphere, and existed for the longest period (on the order of 2500 years). If we say that *there is no other continent with as many blank spots in its prehistory,* then by definition Tiahuanaco must be the main key, for the reasons presented above. As the outstanding Bolivian archaeologist, Javier Escalante, wrote (emphasis by me once again):

The Tiwanakans learned to control their

environment and put to use the abundance of water by installing systems for irrigation and drinking. They constructed bridges and roads and paved them with flagstones with the purpose of uniting principal centers. They developed an *advanced* astronomical calendar which they could use to *precisely* determine seasonal changes and days of the solar year (365.24 days!). See for example the astronomical observatories of Kalasasaya and Pachataka, among others.

Some studies of pre-Colombian times affirm that Tiwanaku launched *the first and oldest technological revolution* on the continent. Medicine, cranial operations and the use of quinine required specialists trained in the area. These Tiwanakan "doctors" intensely researched the medicinal properties of multitudes of plants whose benefits are still used today.

Not only did the Tiwanakans develop architecture, engineering, medicine, herbology and other sciences with great success, but they were also able to develop the arts as well. Ceramics, knitting and craftsmanship in precious metals, stone hewing and carving all left marks of their exquisite creative ability.

Above all, it was a political organization of solidarity and reciprocity that allowed the Tiwanakans to perform great work and create a profoundly humanistic society. This is reflected in their refined handling of rocks, as well as in their exceptional pictorial artwork. They left us a cosmic vision of the world: Earth was created for mankind and mankind for the veneration of gods, a concept in which humans, like the planets and stars, were part of a cosmic equilibrium. [34]

They practiced agriculture at an astoundingly high level. They must have had at least basic knowledge of genetic science, as they left over 300 variations of the potato and over 200 variations of corn (maize)![34] Creating them took not only knowledge, but also time. As Escalante wrote:

> In an area that was virtually infertile [recall the altitude], the Tiwanakans created a system for harvesting crops known as "suka kollus," or farming platforms. This revolutionary system resulted in a series of water channels between strips of land. To build the farming platforms, they first placed large rocks onto the land to form a base. On top of these rocks, they placed a layer of clay to waterproof and further support the platform. Then they placed a layer of gravel and then a layer of sand, both of which served as filters for nutrients. The final layer was soil, which was heaped onto the "platform" in the process of digging out the irrigation ditches that lay parallel to the strips of land. The irrigation ditches were filled with water, which created a micro-climate equivalent to that of the lowlands…
>
> This system provided the perfect combination of nutrients, humidity and other elements needed for healthy crops and yielded a harvest *over twenty times* the amount yielded by conventional agricultural methods. Thanks to this technology, several varieties of the potato, oca and tarwi came into existence. These agricultural inventions made it possible for the Tiwanakans to feed their population and ensure the growth and development of their empire. [34]

It's worth bearing in mind that today Bolivia is not self-sufficient in this respect and has to import food.

Their knowledge was apparently quite versatile. I realized that during my second visit, in 2002. Near the famous "Gate of the Sun" stands an inconspicuous stone block, hardly noticed by most tourists, with a strange hole passing through it. At first glance the hole seems conical, but a closer look reveals that it's not entirely symmetrical. This was puzzling, for generally the block looks very precisely cut and polished, evoking something rather elaborate, and one has the same impression of the hole. After a while I realized that a passing guide had noticed my curiosity (I had been circling the stone) and he explained that it's a peculiar communication tool. He pointed at the distant Akapana pyramid (or the modest ruins of it) a couple of hundred meters away and said that there is an identical block in that location; he continued, "if there were somebody there, he would hear what we are talking about." I just couldn't believe it.

I found the following fragment in Escalante's book:

> On the north end are two blocks, the top third of which has an orifice that works as a kind of auditory device. This hole reaches from one end to the other, and when you place your ear on the highest part of the hole, you can listen to conversations or noises produced from far distances. This discovery provokes us to believe that even in pre-Columbian times people had knowledge of acoustic principles. [34]

It's hard not to associate this example with certain Tibetan traditions, where the sound was "mastered," allegedly to levitate and move great stones, or was used to communicate with other entities by altering the brain's natural oscillations. Such a thread repeats itself in the legends of many cultures.

This example of sophistication forces us to reconsider certain "academic truths," such as the one stating they didn't know the wheel in ancient South America. In a footnote to one of Kondratov's books I found a very interesting piece of information, written by a Soviet archaeologist named Nikolai Shirov:

> In Bolivia, close to Tiahuanaco, great stone wheels have been discovered, drilled in their centers, 2.5m in diameter (7' 16"). They probably served the purpose of transporting the heavy stone blocks at constructions. Apparently the main reason for not

using the wheel in South America was the lack of
domesticated draught animals. There are traditions
that the Incas from Peru knew a primitive plough;
admittedly it was humans that were harnessed in
it. It is possible that *iron was known as well;* it
had its local name, "quillas." According to certain
unverified information, somewhere on the shore of
Lake Titicaca were even situated the furnaces for
iron smelting. [3]

The capability of iron smelting (there is no doubt that they
knew iron of meteoritic origin—meteorites often lie exposed in the
desert), and perhaps even steel smelting, would at least partially
explain the precision found in their art of stonecutting, presented
later, that defies any other conventional explanation. This would
produce another mystery, however: how could such a technology
be later forgotten? Tiahuanaco is a perfect illustration of a certain
"challenge" to *all* the theories, namely that it experienced a
period of uncanny technological progress, followed by an equally
unexplainable period of deterioration. To be perfectly frank,
Bolivia itself is an ideal illustration of this phenomenon, going
from the heights of Tiahuanaco to being a country where a large
part of the population is on the edge of starvation, where most of
the women are illiterate, and GDP per capita annually is around
$700.

Anyway, Tiahuanaco seems to be the "top achievement" in a
certain chain, the culmination of a long process. E. W. Middendorf
translates the city's name as "people who came from afar," which
finds full confirmation in our knowledge. Any attempt to explain
the question of its origin without going beyond the generally
accepted theories comes to no avail.

In my research I have tried to draw a clear line between
complete fantasy or "spiritual" explanations, and reasonable
conclusions following from the detailed observations presented
previously (strangely enough, the scientific theories often don't fit
into either category). I will present now the various early concepts,
as a kind of historical background.

As I mentioned, the "riddle" of this place was born pretty

much at the very moment when the first Spanish conquerors were confronted with the ruins. The first explanation provided by the embarrassed Indians certainly contributed to the legend that successively spread around the world and attracted other travelers. At a time when archaeological knowledge and dating were virtually nonexistent, the very fact that the New World could harbor any great culture was foreign; the first theories as to how could arise were often far out and bizarre. Even quite recently a theory has emerged according to which Tiahuanaco was in fact the lost Atlantis! Spectacular, but too simple to be true.

In the 19th century the ruins were visited by the French riddle-hunter, Augustus Le Plongeon. He made some superficial excavations and, after finding a layer containing what appeared to be seashells, came to the conclusion that Tiahuanaco have once been a sea port and therefore it certainly is "antediluvian." This vision has turned out to be surprisingly long-lived.

After Le Plongeon, another wave of interest—and publications—came in the first decades of the 20th century. Slightly more thorough research was carried out by an American of German origin, Arthur Poznansky, who spent around thirty years of his life trying to resolve the riddle. He too claimed that Tiahuanaco is antediluvian and was a sea lagoon when it was raised to its current elevation. Of course, from today's perspective it's easy to deprecate and rudicule this postulation, nevertheless Poznansky did a great job in gathering quite a lot of information, including some oral traditions, and making the first plans of the site. We may ridicule the idea of a sea lagoon, although in this controversial way he pointed out the unusual fact that the ruins are sorrounded by ancient canals. These are presently dry, and some 20 kilometers away from Lake Titicaca. Moreover, they are slightly inclined to the present surface of the lake! His interpretation was wrong, but the facts are still puzzling indeed.

Both Le Plongeon and Poznansky, as well as many other amateur researchers who followed, unanimously questioned the real age of the ruins. Poznansky managed to popularize the idea that it was "the oldest city on Earth," and with origins officially dated back to around 1500 B.C., *it's the oldest such center of civilization in the entire western hemisphere* (at least 1300 years older than the oldest Mayan ruins, for example).

But is it possible that it is even older?

While there is no solid proof, it is very possible. This is due to the fact that the sediments have not been examined down to the deepest layer. There was a much older material found, possibly from 17th-18th century B.C., that (as is very often the case) archaeologists are not convinced that it was man-made. There are many accounts stating that remains of human bones were occasionally found deeper than the archaeologists excavated, a *lot* deeper. For example: south of the complex, a 3 m (10 ft.) deep layer of bones was discovered by some workers, but the stratigraphy was "disturbed," which disqualified the site for archaeologists; the bones were mixed with various sediments from the lake. What's more intriguing is that there were not only human bones, but also bones representing certain extinct species. This gave rise to the theory that Tiahuanaco fell victim to some unknown cataclysm. This seems justified and even likely. It could be, for instance, a tsunami wave that caused such a disaster: tectonically the area is still very active and earthquakes are nothing exceptional. Later, during the construction of the railway line from La Paz, once again a very thick, grey layer full of bone fragments was encountered. The workers were unable to ascertain the depth to which this layer reached. Because this occured a long time before radiocarbon dating was invented, there was no scientific examination and the whole case was effectively forgotten. So it is possible that the place was inhabited much earlier, but the traces have been "obscured" by geological activity, such as mentioned above, and by the very fact that apparently in ancient times the lakeshore was much closer.

Poznansky was the first to notice, after mapping the ancient, presently barely visible canals, that the city was surrounded by water on all sides, as if once it was a port protruding into the lake. This gave rise to the idea that one may try dating the city (or ascertaining when it started its carreer as a port) by dating the ancient shoreline, to the time when it matched the level of the canals. It seemed this would be relatively easy; no one suspected that it would start quite a strange chain of events and produce quite a strange story.

Scientists have proposed a logical theory that the canals

probably weren't built for ships, but rather to sustain agriculture at this extreme altitude. When one walks around in the midday sun, it's usually comfortably warm—after all it's only 17° from the equator. The air, however, is so thin that immediately after sunset the temperature drops very sharply and the soil would freeze in the absence of water, in whatever form. Regardless of the actual purpose of the canals, the assumption remained valid that determining when the lake reached the canals could be a way of dating the ruins.

Meanwhile, a closer look at the vicinity revealed indications that the end of the "Golden Era" must have had a rather sudden character. As on Easter Island, there were numerous large stone blocks just abandoned in various phases of cutting. Some finished ones were apparently left , on the way. Many lay on the slopes of the nearby Quiappa volcano.

The old shoreline was also clearly visible, as if the change came almost overnight. It was plotted on a map and with this came the first surprise. It turned out that the old shore was significantly inclined to the present level; 0.1-0.15° may not seem much, but in the scale of the entire lake the difference amounts to around 1000 feet (300 m). It appeared, moreover, that the old coastline doesn't form a closed loop, but is open on the south; it simply ends, some distance from the ruins. In other words, had the lake's surface been that much higher, its waters would have spilled over the southern part of the altiplano, towards Lake Poopo; there was no natural barrier. But there must have been something! The only reasonable explanation in this situation was that there must have been a glacier, which could stop the waters. No one knew how long ago such conditions existed, but it was a kind of confirmation that the ruins were indeed quite old. The entire area was clearly shaped by glaciers in some remote past, and the Andes still possess large glaciers; among others the largest permanent ice mass on Earth outside the polar areas is there—the Gran Campo del Hielo in the south of Argentina and Chile.

This finding also suggested that when Tiahuanaco was established the conditions were even harsher and the climate colder, therefore the building of such canals was more important than it would be today. The lake must have been larger than it is presently; now the ancient ditches and canals are on a dry steppe. On the surrounding hills, traces of ancient terraces are visible, but currently no crop cultivation is possible, simply because the climate is too dry. After more careful consideration it turned out, however, that being in the neighborhood of a glacier didn't necessarily imply overall lower temperatures. It recalls the results of a study simulating the North American climate during the time of the last glaciation (some 12,000 years ago), where it was proved that, despite generally lower temperatures, the climate in the immediate vicinity of the glacier was much milder than it is today. The ice mass acted pretty much like a mass of water, stabilizing the temperature throughout the year, making the climate more maritime and less continental. Paradoxically then, the choice to build at such an "inhospitable" place as Tiahuanaco, may not have been that strange. The neighborhood of a glacier would even be beneficial for agriculture. The surface of the lake would be then at the altitude of around 3840m, and not 3812 as it is today.

All that may be just a sidetrack, not very interesting, but it is quite a solid piece of evidence that in spite of the archaeological explanations, the place is still mysterious; there are still questions without answers and its age in particular is not that certain. After all, if people could create a rural and "sedentary" society in South America as long ago as 33,000 years (almost three times older than the end of the Ice Age!), then why shouldn't they build a city 20,000 years later?

That's not the only "indirect" evidence for the extreme antiquity of this place.

It may seem strange, but on the front of the Gate of the Sun there is something that resembles elephant heads. A couple of hundred meters away there stands a statue known as "Benett's monolith" which has quite clear bas-reliefs of *mastodons*. It is known that both these species once existed in South America, but *they died out shortly after the end of the Ice Age*. In the mastodon's case it was around 10,400 years ago (no "younger" fossils have been found). Images of elephants are known from other parts of the Americas as well! There was, for example, a stele at Copan with such detailed heads of American elephants that there was no shadow of a doubt as to their identity. Unfortunately, the stele doesn't exist anymore. In the Museo de Oro (or Museum of Gold) in Colombia's capital, Bogota, I personally saw small sculptures portraying heads of American elephants, so detailed that again any doubt would be out of place. They were apparently made of ivory. I have included a photo of one of them.

After these disquisitions however, it's high time to describe Tiahuanaco itself a little bit more precisely, all the more in that it's only an introduction to the even more interesting place associated with it, nearby Puma Punku.

The largest and most puzzling construction at Tiahuanaco is probably the Akapana pyramid. Its outline has the shape of a sixteen-sided figure and probably portrays half of the "Andean cross." Its horizontal dimensions are 210 by 210 meters (630 feet square). It was built on the basis of a natural mound, around 18m high (over 50 feet) and formed like a stepped pyramid (although in fact it more resembles the stepped stone platforms from Polynesia). Originally it was lined with large, precisely cut stone blocks, but with few exceptions they were removed by the Spaniards and used to raise new buildings, bridges, churches and even to pave roads in La Paz. I once again refer to Escalante's work:

> During the 18th century the Spaniards accidentally excavated the "Piramide de Akapana," while digging for treasures. Akapana is a pyramid–shaped construction of seven stepped terraces… Once its entrance was flanked by sculptures of "Puma Man" (Chachapuma), carved out of black basalt on top of pedestals. According to chronicles, there used to be beautiful structures on top of the pyramid, as well as an *underground temple* with a base in the shape of the Andean step-shaped cross. Unfortunately, when the temple was found, it was already in ruins…
>
> The civic–ceremonial area of Tiwanaku is the most important part of Tiwanaku's culture and of its main city. The most noteworthy structures are: Kalasasaya, Templete Semisubterraneo, Kantatayita, the Akapana Pyramid, Pumapunku,

Karikala and Putuni. Tiwanaku's Regional Museum exhibits some of the more important collections from the area. Among them are beautiful ceramics, lithic and metallic pieces, artifacts made of bones, and human remains that were recovered in various scientific excavations.

Like all the temples in Tiwanaku, *Kalasasaya,* or the Temple of the Stones Standing Up, is also astronomically situated. "Kala" means stone and "Saya" or "Sayasta," straight or standing up. The purpose of this monument was to indicate the change of seasons and the solar year of 365.24 days. In each of the equinox periods (Fall—March 21 and Spring—September 21), the Sun rises through the main entrance. During the Winter Solstice (June 21), the Sun rises in the northeast corner. Similarly, the sunrise in the southeast corner marks the Summer Solstice (December 21)…

The Templete Semisubterraneo (*Semi-Subterranean Temple*) is one of the most decorated constructions of the Golden Age of Tiwanaku. It is located at about two meters below the rest of the constructions in the surrounding area. The foundation is almost a perfect square. Distributed throughout the foundation are 57 supporting pillars made of red sandstone and ashlar. The pillars inside the temple are adorned with 175 transfixed limestone sculptures. Each of the sculptures represents a head completely different from the others.

It is important to note that the water drainage system in this temple, made out of stone channels with a *perfect* decline of 2%, *is still working to date!*

Embedded in the temple's floor was the most impressive anthropomorphic sculpture of the area called Pachamama Monolito (Mother Earth Monolith), also known as Benett's Monolith. Since 1932 the original has stood in front of the stadium in the city of La Paz (in the neighbourhood of Miraflores), although it is now in the process of being returned to its original home.

Kantatayita or "Luz del Amanecer" (Dawn's Light) is a structure with a rectangular base, where we find a renowned lintel with an arc in low relief. The arc is carefully elaborated with carvings depicting the famous Andean step–shaped cross...

Putuni, or Putuputuni (Where the Holes Are), also known as the "Sarcophagus Palace" has a rectangular base with a platform 1.2 meters high. The internal walls hide mortuary chambers with access to the main patio. Of most interest in these chambers is their enclosure system composed of "sliding doors" of stone, that slid across humid floors.

The entrance is a stone-carved stairway that leads to a portal (now dismantled). Underneath the western platform, about two meters down, are dispersion channels. It is probable that these channels were used to drain sewage, which is another indication of how advanced these peoples were in hydraulics and architecture.

A *very strange* archaeological piece [artifact] was found in the immediate area of the civic ceremonial area of Tiwanaku. It involves a type of fired adobe, with colorful decorations. This finding leads us to believe that many other similar works had delicate and elegant finishings. Likewise, in many remains we see low-relief icons with fragments of gold nails, which reveal the way in which these pieces were covered. It must have been a remarkable sight to see the first rays of the Sun shining on these magnificent structures covered with gold plating. All this stands in total contrast to the remains of today, examples of vandalism of the pillagers and religious zealots who destroyed the city...

The Tiwanakans had a notion that the open-aired temples were complete and complex microcosms *created specifically for communication with the gods.* The divine entities of the Tiwanaku religion were found in three levels: sky, Earth and underground. The sky gods resided in the Alakpacha, then there were gods that existed in the Acapacha—the land of living beings, and finally the gods of the underworlds lived in Manquepacha. The pyramidal structures of Akapana and Pumapunku symbolize these three marked levels of Tiwanakan theology. [34]

Certainly not the largest, but one of the greatest objects in Tiahuanaco, made of a single stone block of andesite (around 10 tons, 3 by 3.8 m (9 by 12 feet)), is the famous *Gate of the Sun* or Puerta del Sol. On its pediment there is a frieze, a relief, whose skillful interpretation gives us very significant information about its creators.

The central part of the frieze is occupied by a figure known as the "Crying Viracocha," being a personification of the Sun god, hence the name of the Gate. The Gate occupied a central place in the complex; it was the eastern entrance to the Kalasasaya temple. The central figure stands on top of a step-like platform (which resembles the platforms from Polynesia, but the three steps may also represent the three levels of divine order or levels of enlighment, like in Hindu theology). Viracocha is surrounded by figures of "bird-men" that seem to adore him. The "bird-men" standing upright hold objects that resemble sticks or bars, just like in the Rongo-Rongo writing.

Viracocha himself is a mysterious figure, by the way. Supposedly he was a human personification of a god who arrived by sea from the Pacific, and taught the Indians how to build civilization. Nothing unusual, but strange is the fact that contrary to other religious icons, he doesn't resemble the Indians themselves. According to the traditions he was bearded, had white skin, a long nose and so on; Lima's museums contain plenty of sculptures of him. Tane, the other god, also didn't fit the scheme.

According to the German anthropologist Paul Herrmann and the New Zealander, Professor Peter H. Buck, he was "the protector of craftsmen and dexterity, the god and forefather of white people."[5] Quite strange, isn't it?

All the peculiarities of Tiahuanaco fade, however, in the light of the nearby complex of ruins known as *Puma Punku* (considered part of Tiahuanaco by some). It's around 800m (or half a mile) away. Puma Punku, despite the spatial proximity, is *something completely different,* at least in respect to the part of Tiahuanaco which can be seen today. The latter, although constituting ruins, "stands normally," to put it as straighforwardly as possible. The sections of walls which survived the ransacking of the Spaniards are not destroyed, whereas at Puma Punku there are indications that some tumultuous event rsulted in its ruination. With regard to Tiahuanaco, the Spanish couldn't imagine how human hands could raise such a complex, and they considered it therefore a creation of Satan. They not only used the blocks at their own construction sites—to build churches in particular—but also tried to destroy anything they weren't able to move, mostly the statues, by testing cannonballs on them, for example.

Puma Punku is such an unusual place, viewed from the context of our entire planet, that it seems to be something from beyond our space and time. The precision of stonecutting visible here and the level of its complexity are *evident* remains of some technological civilization's activity. I have seen in my life a lot of ruins and other traces from the remote past, left over by various cultures, but Puma Punku made a colossal impression on me, to such an extent that when I saw it for the first time in 1997, unprepared, I promised myself that someday I would return to document it, with a good video and adequate measuring equipment, adequate to the level of precision. That was my dream. It was supposed to be a well-planned expedition.

An opportunity emerged in March 2002, when I got a ticket to Santiago de Chile. Only 2000 km divided the Chilean capital from my "target." Luckily, the flight on the modern A-320 of LAN-Chile turned out to be completely opposite to my earlier experience in Ecuador.

There were however certain problems, although of a different nature. They resulted, first of all, from the unimaginable—for a European—altitude of the Andean plateau. The plane made a stopover in the north of Chile, in Iquique, and the final leg of flight was to take merely 20 minutes. Usually, shortly after takeoff the pressure inside the cabin is reduced (in order to reduce the load acting on the skin plating) to a pressure equivalent to that at 2000–2500m above the sea level (6500–8200 ft.). Normally it's very bearable, but in this case, due to the short time of flight, the pilot reduced it more and quicker. Within around ten minutes it dropped to around half of the atmospheric pressure at sea level! The El Alto airport near La Paz was then—until some Tibetan airport was opened by the Chinese—the highest one in the world: 4050m (or 13,300 feet) above sea level. That's a life threatening problem for some. At first you just feel the lack of oxygen; more serious symptoms usually come at night, but for some older passengers simply carrying luggage was apparently a challenge, and some needed immediate medical assistance. I managed to cope with the problem, at least for a while, by using a method well proven by the Incas: the so called "mate de coca." Just after getting to the hotel, I imbibed this tea made of coca leafes. It's safe to drink, resembles green tea, only that everything sways before your eyes. Even although I am quite healthy, the very intensive work in Puma Punku two days later almost killed me; my eyes turned red, my nose was bleeding and I had clear pre-heart attack symptoms. I'm not writing this because I expect sympathy on the reader's part, but somebody who has not experienced this will hardly understand how big a question mark is the fact that such an unbelievable civilization emerged in this place and then overshadowed everything else in the entire hemisphere.

In the case of the visible part of Tiahuanaco there are no noticeable traces of any serious cataclysm, or of *any* cataclysm. Puma Punku, however, which is a large complex, seems as if it was turned upside down and mixed with the ground; at the time of discovery it was basically a mound of ground and chaotically dispersed, machined (?) stone blocks. *When one looks at the toppled fragments of a once gigantic stone platform weighing over 1000 tons, it becomes obvious that human hands could not cause this destruction.* A conclusion follows from this observation that

213

Puma Punku may be older than Tiahuanaco itself.

Even a brief look at some of the extremely precisely carved blocks indicates that Puma Punku's creators possessed a technology of a much higher level, than in the case of the nearby Tiahuanaco (which nonetheless displays amazing amazing achievements in the art of stonecutting), which must be very highly assessed even according to our contemporary standards. Looking at the site we have the overwhelming impression that we deal here with a *backward development* from an advanced, sophisticated technology in the most remote past, through moderately developed technology in nearer history, up to its almost complete atrophy presently.

When taking into account modern construction achievements, we face the truth that *many of the construction methods that were applied in Puma Punku have absolutely no equivalent anywhere else in the world and would even be hard to reproduce in our time.*

A serial stonecutting of the blocks (of very hard andesite) was applied, characterized by a precision hardly achievable even today! I cannot imagine a contemporary designer who would propose to build some large object of megalithic blocks having such complex shapes, reproduced with a precision of the order of one tenth of a milimeter (which is roughly the thickness of this sheet of paper), while the convex edges, formed by merging surfaces made with such a precision were to correspond with analogous concave two- or three-dimensional edges of other blocks. Such a designer would have to be crazy! But such precision can be found at Puma Punku!

The cutting machines currently in use (millers, for example) with rotating tools do not enable us to make such sharp concave edges, and in particular such sharp three dimensional concave corners merging three perpendicular surfaces—not to mention the serial production of them! Such a technology simply does not exist. You can make a precise surface and polish it, or connect two such surfaces with a convex or concave edge, but it would be quite a challenge to connect *three* such surfaces and create a 90° concave corner, still keeping the 0.1mm precision tolerance in the very corner! I'm not aware of such a technology.

The only thing that could theoretically make it possible is

casting, but it seems very unlikely that this was used at Puma Punku. First of all it would take a very high temperature, and taking into account the overall size of the blocks (large), combined with their "thinness" in some cases, the main problem would be the potential breaking of the blocks during cooling; they would have to be cooled very slowly for days, in special furnaces. There is also certain direct evidence that the most challenging blocks were *not* cast. Andesite and plutonite—the most often used rocks—are volcanic; they are a certain kind of solidified lava, and as such they contain small bubbles of gas. When I looked at these blocks it was clearly visible that the lenticular bubbles they contain are parallel. At the ends of the blocks they are often cut in two, which suggests that machining they were already in the rock bfore it was cut. Another evidence is that in the case of casting the bubbles would not be parallel, but rather they would "radiate" from the center in all directions. Casting may therefore be ruled out. Apart from the matter of the bubbles, I cannot believe that casting would produce such precise edges. After all, even molten lava is relatively dense; it would have to be a very high pressure casting. The main problem in this scenario is that often the shapes are simply too complex.

In Puma Punku there are whole *series* of identical complex blocks. The H-letter type blocks have almost 80 surfaces each! I suspect that a contemporary engineer could not even imagine designing them without a computer. From the point of view of our perception of prehistory, this precision constitutes a very serious challenge, as serious as the existence of the geographically correlated points along the "Axis of the World." And it seems there is a lack of interest on the part of science in taking up this challenge and attempting to incorporate these facts into the existing theories; that's just not possible.

Particularly large and heavy blocks at Puma Punku were connected by using metal clamps. In each block that was to be connected, a concave profile or carving was made, usually u-shaped or t-shaped, after which they were filled with liquid copper. After solidifying it formed a strong and rigid connection. Such a method created a junction resistant to transverse loads, which in this context means that it could survive an earthquake. Despite the extreme altitude such tremors are not unusual there; the Andes are young mountains, still uplifting.

Examination of the blocks reveals also the use of one more unconventional technology. In some places one can observe groups (usually rows) of very precisely made holes. The precision is so great that it *rules out* manual processing. First and foremost, they generally have exactly the same diameter, the sides are very smooth (if the holes are not damaged, of course) and precisely parallel. The deviations in this respect—i.e., differences of the diameter between the top and bottom of the hole—are on the order of 0.1mm. This corresponds with drilling by a machine fixed on some mount, for it could not be done by holding the tool in one's hands, especially working a very hard stone. Recognizing this level of technology required to produce these blocks, and then realizing the official theories, according to which these people didn't even know the wheel, can cause one's head to spin!

One example of this technology is represented by the cuboidal, standing upright block, shown in enclosed photographs. On one of its sides was made (milled?) a precise groove having a semi-elliptical cross section, 4.5mm wide and around 1m long (I will use only the decimal system of measures in this part of the book, as it is much easier to calculate). In it, distanced by around 28 mm (but this dimension is not precisely maintained), a row of holes was made, having a diameter slightly less than that of the groove itself. My measurements from 2002 revealed that all the holes have the same diameter (4.0mm) and the deviations measured at a certain depth do not exceed 0.1mm. Even a quick glance at the ideally straight, undamaged edge of the groove, or the perfectly flat external surfaces of the block, removes any doubt that it was *extremely sophisticated machining* that was used here. I have put a caliper's arm (which is very precise) to this surface when the sun was in the background and one could see, that there is no light shining through whatsoever. I wouldn't have been able to put a hair in the "gap." In fact, I couldn't see anything! No radiocarbon datings have been made directly at this site, but scientists estimate that the ruins are approximately 1500 years old. No wonder then that certain blocks have damaged edges, although their condition is amazingly good. Perhaps the very fact that they were buried has restricted erosion. I have to repeat that although I have seen numerous ruins during various trips, I have never encountered anything even comparable to Puma Punku. There is no other place, anywhere, where hard, large blocks are carved in such a complex way.

From skeptical scientists, the "debunkers," we often hear that all the wonders of prehistoric construction were accomplished only very simple stone or copper hand tools, accessible to primitive peoples. I would propose to chain such a scholar to a comparatively hard and large stone block, along with such primitive tools, until he turned it into a block such as as one just described. But there would be an additional surprise adding to the difficulty level: the block has a circular hole on its upper surface which fluently turns inside the stone and comes out from the side as a hollow with a square cross section!

It would be rather hard to imagine such hollows serving as connections with other blocks; the resistance of such a connections would probably be too low. They could, however, be used to fix some mechanisms, installations or simply decorative elements, although nothing of this kind has been found so far. For this reason, and because many of the blocks seem to have been abandoned, not having been assembled into any object or building, there is the assumption that the place was destroyed before the works were finished. It's worth adding that according to the local legends, it was destroyed by Viracocha with "deadly rays" before the deluge.

My main objective during my trip in 2002 was to carry out precise measurements. The most important observations didn't require any sophisticated equipment or preparations; the precision itself is clearly visible. A video camera was sufficient in this respect. Another piece of information I wanted to obtain was the unit of length that was used by the builders. This wasn't a serious challenge, either. To this end it was enough just to measure the dimensions and compare them with each other in order to find instances of recurrence, and especially the most often appearing common multiples of the dimensions. The goals in this case were simple but significant: firstly, I wanted to compare the unit with that used at Tiahuanaco, and secondly, it should provide a clear and reliable bit of information as to the origins of the creators. I hoped that perhaps it would be a unit used somewhere else in the world and in this case the information would enable us to connect Puma Punku with some other culture, to place it within some context. After all, the fact that the site has no equivalent even in South America must be seen as strange; it's an isolated example that seems to emerge out of nothing.

Not all the blocks at Puma Punku are cut so precisely as the one I have decribed in detail, but I concentrated on the ones that are relatively undamaged and that display state-of-the-art technology. I started with a block whose particular design appeared on only one other block. I found replicability of the 50mm dimension (deviation on the order of 0.05 mm—which turned out to be the smallest throughout the place) and perfect replicability of the 62.7mm dimension (+/- 0.1 mm). Longer dimensions, such as the overall dimensions, were harder to measure precisely because, as in the case of other blocks, this one had slightly chipped external edges, and apart from that it was broken.

I was very curious how the more complex, but also more timeworn, "H-type" blocks would hold up under this scrutiny. I made a series of measurements, some of which are indicated on a drawing. The width between the most distant external edges was around 877mm. Within a given block it was rather constant, but between various blocks of the same type it differed slightly. generally by the order of 1mm (so the blocks measured between 876–878 mm). A shorter dimension I tested fluctuated similarly. Within the lot it was 249–250 mm, although to some extent the variation was the result of damage along the edges.

Already based on this data it is possible to notice a *specific unit of length,* the simplest multiplication. Because the most precise measurements of the first block were the starting point and best reference, one may presume that it is 125.4mm. If we divide all the above values by this peculiar unit, we get the following fractions: 0.500 (62.7 mm divided by 125.4), 0.399 (dividing 50 mm), 6.99 (dividing 877 mm) and 1.99 (dividng 249 mm). This rule was verified positively practically everywhere—for example the block standing upright, described earlier (with the precise groove and holes 4.00 mm in diameter) is 873 mm high, although it may be slightly more because its "bottom" is significantly damaged. This value produces a result of 6.96 when divided. Its width measures almost 381mm (3.03). As can be seen, exceptions to the rule are very rare and generally do not exceed 1%—especially in the case of relatively undamaged edges. I have noticed that the multiplication of 7 units and 3.5 units occurs more often than others.

I intended to compare these results with measurements from Tiahuanaco; but it turned out that it's very hard to find anything there with even comparably precise surfaces, and therefore to obtain comparably precise lengths. In this respect these are two different worlds, with a few exceptions of course. While passing close to the Gate of the Sun, I spotted such an exception; almost instinctively, I saw that it didn't match the rest. It was distinctive in that it looked like an ideal cuboid. I was even happier to note that it's practically undamaged. I have named it "the measurement standard." I measured its length and width—the rule aplied to it as well. It was respectively 1375 and 1065 mm, therefore approximately 11 and 8.5 units (or precisely: 10.97 and 8.49—with a precision of 99.7% and 99.9%). The third dimension—the height—turned out however to be a problem. It was 197 mm.

In no way did this match the aforementioned unit of length! As a result of dividing by 125.4 we get 1.5709. It was the first case where a value contradicted the other measurements. Even if we were to assume that it was supposed to be 1.5, an unprecedented deviation of 7% would remain. Intuitively, I did then something that would appear illogical: I pulled out my calculator and multiplicated the errant value of 1.5709 by two, not knowing specifically why. The digits presented *a true revelation: 3.1418! The π number! Unbelievable!* It differed from the ideal (3.1416) only by 0.0002. It is, as far as I know, only one of two representations of the π number from the ancient world, and it's definitely the most precise one—the seemingly perfect Egyptians used an approximation in the form of the fraction 22/7 —therefore 3.1429 (with a deviation of 0.0013). We can announce therefore of a true sensation—in the sea of ignorance in which Puma Punku is submerged.

The existence of this "sea" means also that the numerical relations from Puma Punku do not reach the so-called "authorities." There are no theories worked out, either about the role of this place, or regarding *the purpose* of such precise stonecutting (let

219

alone the technology itself!). It gets a certain amount of attention only in Bolivian archaeology, mostly because the entire complex is the main archaeological asset of this country, and it's not very far from the capital, which is an academic center. There is also the work if Ibarra Grasso, only it has been almost forgotten. In connection with these facts, the only meaningful reflections on the character and purpose of Puma Punku are found in the work cited earlier by the leading Bolivian archaeologist. Apparently he was unaware of any actual mathematical analysis of the blocks (probably nobody did it before), but perhaps thanks to this, his "predictions" are all the more interesting:

> The people of Tiwanaku had a special interest in going beyond the limits of temporality. Preoccupied by the inevitable transformation determined by sacred forces, they left *special messages* via discriminating carvings of mathematic and geometric origins. The "Gateway of the Sun" is a clear example of the high level of science they were able to reach. Diverse studies attribute this work to be a function of communication, for *messages left for the future.* There are numerous works in stone with fine carvings, as if these people wanted their messages to be eternal.
>
> Earlier it was believed that these carvings were only for aesthetic purposes, with the function of decorating existing pieces. Recent studies, however, show that said signs were previously designed and planned before being worked in stone and that they contained messages of a mathematical and geometrical nature... Studies of these signs still continue and each time the results are more convincing. The time will come when these "messages for eternity" can be deciphered... [34]

They have left encoded information for future generations so that, after achieving a certain level of consciousness, these generations could some day learn the real history of our planet!

220

I'm sure that a larger-scale project could bring other discoveries. First of all, the excavations in Puma Punku should be finished, as well as the research *on the bottom* of Lake Titicaca (described by David Hatcher Childress, among others). There lie mysterious ruins which could contribute to the solution of this riddle, discovered in the 1960s near Puerto Acosta by the American William Mardoff. The find was confirmed shortly after that by an Argentine expedition of Ramon Avellaneda and then by another North American group. In August 2000 an Italian expedition called "Atahuallpa 2000" headed by Lorenzo Epis and cooperating with Bolivian archaeologists, discovered, among other things, the ruins of a giant temple on the bottom of this lake. The temple is 200m long, 50m wide and was surrounded by a wall, a fragment of which was recorded by the expedition on film. The wall is 800m long—half a mile! It's hard not to make an analogy with Nan Madol…

But regardless of the significance of these facts, there is one more far-reaching conclusion following from the analysis presented above. One of the questions mentioned earlier still remains unanswered: has the unit of measurement from Puma Punku enabled us to link it with any other culture? Was it used anywhere else? The answer is startling indeed. The value of 125.4 mm is precisely one fourth of the so-called Sumerian "ell" (502 mm). This is a clear indication that the Protodravidian civilization had something to do with that early people. As we remember, the Sumerians migrated there through the sea from the east—I think we can safely say from the Indus Valley! After all, it was closely tied with the Sumer and besides, it would be quite hard to find any alternative explanation. We shouldn't forget however, that the similarity of calendars in both Peru and Sumer was already suspicious. One might expect in this light that their methods and units of calculation might also have been similar as a whole.

I suspect that Puma Punku is the most interesting of all the riddles presented in this book, but the data revealed in the course of the research there would seem virtually meaningless (perhaps even silly or unbelievable) outside the context of the Axis as a whole, described in the previous chapters. This context enables us to see this crowning achievement as a consequence of a complex process. It served this purpose.

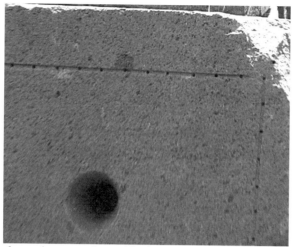

Drill holes and saw marks on blocks at Puma Punku. Despite erosion, the precision is plain to see. One cannot do something like this without precise tools!

Blocks at Puma Punku. These H-type blocks have over 80 surfaces.

Drill holes and saw marks on blocks at Puma Punku. They must have been drilled with a tool with a precisely stabilized axis – the rock is brittle and any wobbling would have left visible traces. It was a technological civilization – and this is the material evidence!

Damaged blocks at Puma Punku. They demonstrate most clearly the concave connections of three surfaces perpendicular to one other, where even the very corners have no visible arcs or curves – they are precise to the order of 0.1 mm.

223

H-type blocks at Puma Punku.

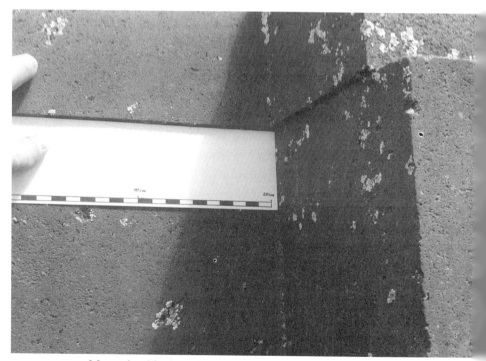

Measuring blocks at Puma Punku.

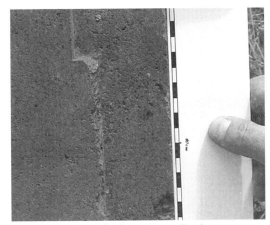

Measuring blocks at Puma Punku.

H-type blocks at Puma Punku.

The trapezoid-inset-type block at Puma Punku.

Measuring blocks at Puma Punku.

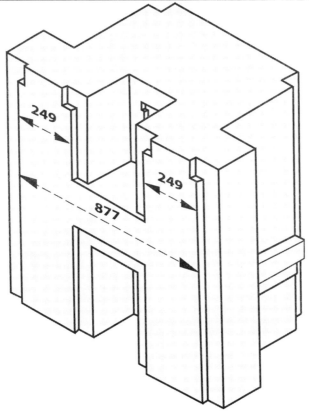

Blocks at Puma Punku.

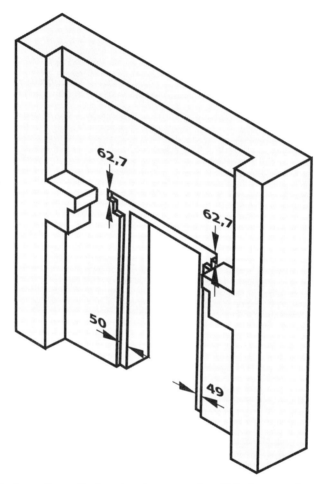

Blocks at Puma Punku. Another example of blocks manufactured serially. Some measurements of the most significant blocks. Dimensions in mm (by I. Witkowski).

Bibliography and Endnotes

1. F. Maziere. *Fantastique Ile de Paques*. Publ. Laffont 1965.
2. A. Kondratov. *Zaginione cywilizacje* (*Lost Civilizations*). Warsaw 1983.
3. A. Kondratov. *Tajemnice trzech oceanow* (*Mysteries of Three Oceans*). Warsaw 1980.
4. T. Heyerdahl. *Iskusstvo Ostrova Paschi* (*The Art of Easter Island*) Soviet edition. Publ. Iskusstvo 1982.
5. P. Herrmann. *Sieben vorbei und acht verweht*. Berlin. 1965.
6. P. H. Buck. *Vikings of the Pacific*. (Quotations translated from Polish edition) Warsaw. 1983.
7. B. Zb. Szalek. *Korzenie Wyspy Wielkanocnej* (*The Roots of Easter Island*). Szczecin University. 1995.
8. B. Zb. Szalek. *The Narmini report – Vol. 1: Decipherement of the Easter Island Script; Vol. 2: Decipherement of the Indus Valley Script.* 1999.
9. B. Zb. Szalek. "Linguistic evidence for a prehistoric Eurasian empire of „3 races and 1 language". *Journal of the Oriental Institute M. S. University of Baroda* (India). March – June 1998.
10. B. Zb. Szalek. "On the Dravidian Axis 27N – 27S (Mohenjo Daro – Easter Island)". *Journal of the Oriental Institute M. S. University of Baroda* (India). September – December 1997.
11. B. Zb. Szalek. "The Axis 27N – 27S as a geographic proof...". *Migration and Diffusion*. Vol. 1/2000.
12. S. N. Kramer. *Die Geschichte beginnt in Sumer*. Polish Edition Warsaw. 1961.
13. E. Stucken. "Polynesisches Sprachgut in Amerika und in Sumer". *Mitteilungen der Vorderasiatisch-Aegyptischen Gesellschaft*. Berlin. 1926.
14. Z. Skrok. *Kto odkry Ameryke?* (*Who Discovered America?*). Warsaw. 1987.
15. M. Parfit. „Wkraczaja pierwsi Amerykanie" ("The First Americans are Coming") Polish edition of *National Geographic Magazine*. 12/2000.

16. T. Dillehay. "Monte Verde: A late pleistocene settlement in Chile". Vol 2: *The Archaeological Context*. Smithsonian Institution Press. 1997.
17. *Science,* 2 May 1997.
18. Collective work *Sztuka swiata. Vol. 1* (*Art of the World – Ssupplement to the Polish Edition*). Warsaw. 1989.
19. M. Coe, et al. *Atlas of Ancient America*. Oxford. 1990.
20. K. Piasecki. "Kim byli pierwsi mieszkancy Nowego Swiata?" ("Who were the First Inhabitants of the New World?"). *Swiat Nauki* (Warsaw) No. 11/2000.
21. David Hatcher Childress. *Lost Cities of Ancient Lemuria and the Pacific*". Kempton, Illinois. Adventures Unlimited Press.
22. T. Heyerdahl.. *The Maldive Mystery*. Bethesda. 1986.
23. E. Dzikowska. *Limanskie ABC* (*ABC of Lima*). Warsaw 1982.
24. "Polynesians and Amerinds". *Archaeology*, November/ December 1996.
25. J. M. Cruxent. "Notes on Venezuelan Archaeology". Part of *Indian Tribes of Aboriginal America*. Chicago 1952.
26. N. Fernandez Naranjo. *Texto elemental de lectura en castellano e aymara....* La Paz, Bolivia. 1954.
27. N. M. Holmer, et al. "A Modelled Picture Writing from the Kechua Indians." *Ethnos*. 1951.
28. R. J. Hunt. *Mataco Grammar*. Universidad Nacional de Tucuman. 1940.
29. D. E. Ibarra – Grasso. *La escritura indigena Andina*. La Paz, Bolivia. 1953.
30. F. F. Outes. "Un texto Aonukun'k..." *Revista del Museo de La Plata*. Vol. XXI/1928.
31. A. Serrano. "Observaciones sobre El Kakan, el extinguido idioma...". *Boletin de la Academia Argentina de Letras*, vol. IV, No. 14/1936.
32. D. E. Ibarra – Grasso. *Argentina indigena y prehistoria Americana*. Buenos Aires. 1967.
33. L. Znicz. *Goscie z kosmosu? – paleoastronautyka*. Warsaw .1983.
34. J. Escalante. *Tiwanaku – cultural patrimony of humanity*. La Paz, Bolivia. 2001.

35. A. Kondratov. *Lemuria – klucz do przeszlosci* (*Lemuria – the Key to thePast*). Warsaw. 1983.

36. M. Bielicki. *Zapomniany swiat Sumerow*. (*The Forgotten World of the Sumerians*). Warsaw. 1966.

37. M. Keciek – Przeglad Tygodniowy. 17 December 1997.

38. E. O'Brien. "Mystery of the mummies". www.fi.edu/inquirer/mummy.html.

39. J. P. Mallory, V. Mair. "The Tarim Mummies". New York. 2000.

40. A. Nur, Z. Ben-Avraham. "Lost Pacifica continent..." *Nature* 3 Nov. 1977.

41. J. Machowski. *Odkrywanie Ameryki*. Warsaw. 2002.

42. J. Adovasio, J. Page. *The first Americans*. New York. 2002.

43. G. Hancock. *Underworld – Flooded Kingdoms of the Ice Age*. London: Penguin. 2002.

44. T. Dillehay. "Tracking the First Americans". *Nature* 4 Sept. 2003.

45. R. Sternal. „Nanmatol..." *Nieznany Swiat* (Warsaw) No. 2/1993.

46. "Xinjiang Mummies Proved Caucasian." *World Explorer*, Vol. 4, no. 1.

47. V. Domenici, D. Domenici. "Talking Knots of the Inka". *Archaeology*. November/December 1996.

48. M. Ziolkowski. "Przedkolumbijskie pisma peruwianskie". *Z Otchlani Wiekow*, March 1974.

49. A. Kolata. *The Tiwanaku*. Cambridge (USA) 1993.

50. M. Stingl. *Czciciele Gwiazd* (*Worshippers of the Stars*). Warsaw. 1985.

51. J. Churchward, *The Lost Continent of Mu*, New York, 1931.

52. J.M. Brown, *Riddle of the Pacific*, New York, 1924.

A reconstruction of the wall with the Gate of the Sun by early archeologists.

A reconstruction of the walls at Puma Punku by early Bolivian archeologists.

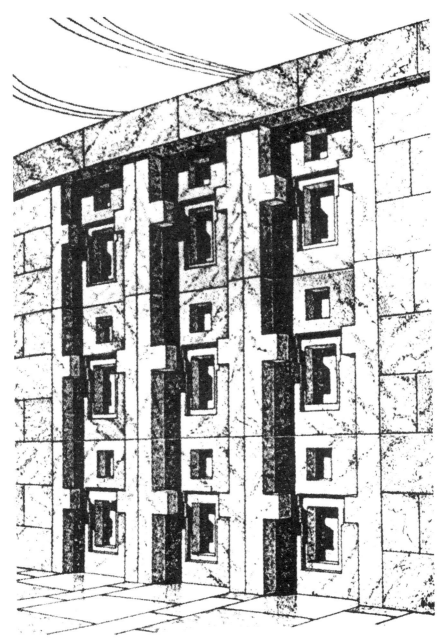

A reconstruction of a wall at Puma Punku using the uniformly cut blocks.

Igor Witkowski measuring blocks at Puma Punku, Bolivia.

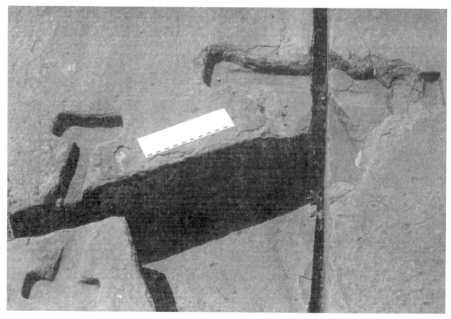

T-shaped keystone cuts on blocks at Puma Punku.

A section of the massive granite blocks at Puma Punku.

Top: A cut for a metal circle clamp at Puma Punku. Below: Another cut for a circular metal clamp with two precision-drilled holes next to it.

236

Top: Scattered blocks at Puma Punku. Below: A square-shaped set of holes and cuts for a clamp on one of the blocks. It's striking when observing the blocks at Puma Punku that the making of various holes was apparently easy for the builders. Some are very precise, despite having a large diameter.

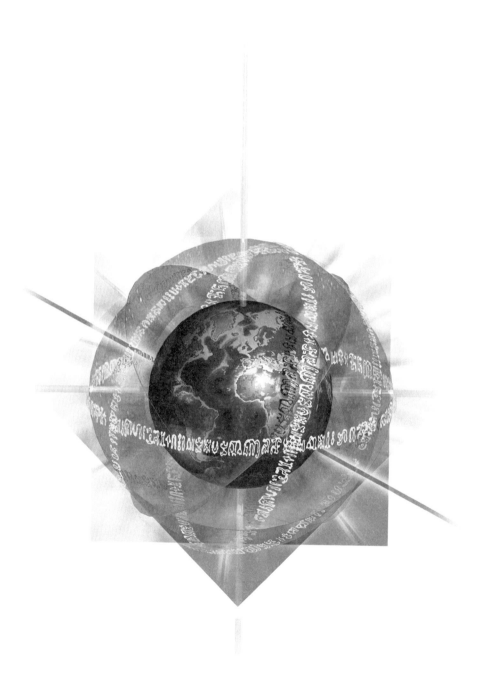

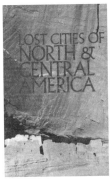

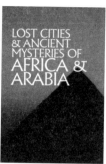

LOST CITIES & ANCIENT MYSTERIES OF AFRICA & ARABIA
by David Hatcher Childress
Childress continues his world-wide quest for lost cities and ancient mysteries. Join him as he discovers forbidden cities in the Empty Quarter of Arabia; "Atlantean" ruins in Egypt and the Kalahari desert; a mysterious, ancient empire in the Sahara; and more. This is the tale of an extraordinary life on the road: across war-torn countries, Childress searches for King Solomon's Mines, living dinosaurs, the Ark of the Covenant and the solutions to some of the fantastic mysteries of the past.
423 PAGES. 6x9 PAPERBACK. ILLUSTRATED. $14.95. CODE: AFA

LOST CITIES OF ATLANTIS, ANCIENT EUROPE & THE MEDITERRANEAN
by David Hatcher Childress
Childress takes the reader in search of sunken cities in the Mediterranean; across the Atlas Mountains in search of Atlantean ruins; to remote islands in search of megalithic ruins; to meet living legends and secret societies. From Ireland to Turkey, Morocco to Eastern Europe, and around the remote islands of the Mediterranean and Atlantic, Childress takes the reader on an astonishing quest for mankind's past. Ancient technology, cataclysms, megalithic construction, lost civilizations and devastating wars of the past are all explored in this book.
524 PAGES. 6x9 PAPERBACK. ILLUSTRATED. $16.95. CODE: MED

LOST CITIES OF CHINA, CENTRAL ASIA & INDIA
by David Hatcher Childress
Like a real life "Indiana Jones," maverick archaeologist David Childress takes the reader on an incredible adventure across some of the world's oldest and most remote countries in search of lost cities and ancient mysteries. Discover ancient cities in the Gobi Desert; hear fantastic tales of lost continents, vanished civilizations and secret societies bent on ruling the world; visit forgotten monasteries in forbidding snow-capped mountains with strange tunnels to mysterious subterranean cities! A unique combination of far-out exploration and practical travel advice, it will astound and delight the experienced traveler or the armchair voyager.
429 PAGES. 6x9 PAPERBACK. ILLUSTRATED. FOOTNOTES & BIBLIOGRAPHY. $14.95. CODE: CHI

LOST CITIES OF ANCIENT LEMURIA & THE PACIFIC
by David Hatcher Childress
Was there once a continent in the Pacific? Called Lemuria or Pacifica by geologists, Mu or Pan by the mystics, there is now ample mythological, geological and archaeological evidence to "prove" that an advanced and ancient civilization once lived in the central Pacific. Maverick archaeologist and explorer David Hatcher Childress combs the Indian Ocean, Australia and the Pacific in search of the surprising truth about mankind's past. Contains photos of the underwater city on Pohnpei; explanations on how the statues were levitated around Easter Island in a clockwise vortex movement; tales of disappearing islands; Egyptians in Australia; and more.
379 PAGES. 6x9 PAPERBACK. ILLUSTRATED. FOOTNOTES & BIBLIOGRAPHY. $14.95. CODE: LEM

A HITCHHIKER'S GUIDE TO ARMAGEDDON
by David Hatcher Childress
With wit and humor, popular Lost Cities author David Hatcher Childress takes us around the world and back in his trippy finalé to the Lost Cities series. He's off on an adventure in search of the apocalypse and end times. Childress hits the road from the fortress of Megiddo, the legendary citadel in northern Israel where Armageddon is prophesied to start. Hitchhiking around the world, Childress takes us from one adventure to another, to ancient cities in the deserts and the legends of worlds before our own. In the meantime, he becomes a cargo cult god on a remote island off New Guinea, gets dragged into the Kennedy Assassination by one of the "conspirators," investigates a strange power operating out of the Altai Mountains of Mongolia, and discovers how the Knights Templar and their off-shoots have driven the world toward an epic battle centered around Jerusalem and the Middle East.
320 PAGES. 6x9 PAPERBACK. ILLUSTRATED. BIBLIOGRAPHY. INDEX. $16.95. CODE: HGA

TECHNOLOGY OF THE GODS
The Incredible Sciences of the Ancients
by David Hatcher Childress
Childress looks at the technology that was allegedly used in Atlantis and the theory that the Great Pyramid of Egypt was originally a gigantic power station. He examines tales of ancient flight and the technology that it involved; how the ancients used electricity; megalithic building techniques; the use of crystal lenses and the fire from the gods; evidence of various high tech weapons in the past, including atomic weapons; ancient metallurgy and heavy machinery; the role of modern inventors such as Nikola Tesla in bringing ancient technology back into modern use; impossible artifacts; and more.
356 PAGES. 6x9 PAPERBACK. ILLUSTRATED. BIBLIOGRAPHY. $16.95. CODE: TGOD

VIMANA AIRCRAFT OF ANCIENT INDIA & ATLANTIS
by David Hatcher Childress, introduction by Ivan T. Sanderson
In this incredible volume on ancient India, authentic Indian texts such as the *Ramayana* and the *Mahabharata* are used to prove that ancient aircraft were in use more than four thousand years ago. Included in this book is the entire Fourth Century BC manuscript *Vimaanika Shastra* by the ancient author Maharishi Bharadwaaja. Also included are chapters on Atlantean technology, the incredible Rama Empire of India and the devastating wars that destroyed it.
334 PAGES. 6x9 PAPERBACK. ILLUSTRATED. $15.95. CODE: VAA

LOST CONTINENTS & THE HOLLOW EARTH
I Remember Lemuria and the Shaver Mystery
by David Hatcher Childress & Richard Shaver
Shaver's rare 1948 book *I Remember Lemuria* is reprinted in its entirety, and the book is packed with illustrations from Ray Palmer's *Amazing Stories* magazine of the 1940s. Palmer and Shaver told of tunnels running through the earth—tunnels inhabited by the Deros and Teros, humanoids from an ancient spacefaring race that had inhabited the earth, eventually going underground, hundreds of thousands of years ago. Childress discusses the famous hollow earth books and delves deep into whatever reality may be behind the stories of tunnels in the earth. Operation High Jump to Antarctica in 1947 and Admiral Byrd's bizarre statements, tunnel systems in South America and Tibet, the underground world of Agartha, the belief of UFOs coming from the South Pole, more.
344 PAGES. 6x9 PAPERBACK. ILLUSTRATED. $16.95. CODE: LCHE

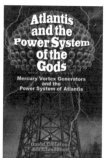

MAPS OF THE ANCIENT SEA KINGS
Evidence of Advanced Civilization in the Ice Age
by Charles H. Hapgood
Charles Hapgood has found the evidence in the Piri Reis Map that shows Antarctica, the Hadji Ahmed map, the Oronteus Finaeus and other amazing maps. Hapgood concluded that these maps were made from more ancient maps from the various ancient archives around the world, now lost. Not only were these unknown people more advanced in mapmaking than any people prior to the 18th century, it appears they mapped all the continents. The Americas were mapped thousands of years before Columbus. Antarctica was mapped when its coasts were free of ice!
316 PAGES. 7x10 PAPERBACK. ILLUSTRATED. BIBLIOGRAPHY & INDEX. $19.95. CODE: MASK

PATH OF THE POLE
Cataclysmic Pole Shift Geology
by Charles H. Hapgood
Maps of the Ancient Sea Kings author Hapgood's classic book *Path of the Pole* is back in print! Hapgood researched Antarctica, ancient maps and the geological record to conclude that the Earth's crust has slipped on the inner core many times in the past, changing the position of the pole. *Path of the Pole* discusses the various "pole shifts" in Earth's past, giving evidence for each one, and moves on to possible future pole shifts.
356 PAGES. 6x9 PAPERBACK. ILLUSTRATED. $16.95. CODE: POP

SECRETS OF THE HOLY LANCE
The Spear of Destiny in History & Legend
by Jerry E. Smith
Secrets of the Holy Lance traces the Spear from its possession by Constantine, Rome's first Christian Caesar, to Charlemagne's claim that with it he ruled the Holy Roman Empire by Divine Right, and on through two thousand years of kings and emperors, until it came within Hitler's grasp—and beyond! Did it rest for a while in Antarctic ice? Is it now hidden in Europe, awaiting the next person to claim its awesome power? Neither debunking nor worshiping, *Secrets of the Holy Lance* seeks to pierce the veil of myth and mystery around the Spear. Mere belief that it was infused with magic by virtue of its shedding the Savior's blood has made men kings. But what if it's more? What are "the powers it serves"?
312 PAGES. 6x9 PAPERBACK. ILLUSTRATED. BIBLIOGRAPHY. $16.95. CODE: SOHL

THE FANTASTIC INVENTIONS OF NIKOLA TESLA
by Nikola Tesla with additional material by
David Hatcher Childress
This book is a readable compendium of patents, diagrams, photos and explanations of the many incredible inventions of the originator of the modern era of electrification. In Tesla's own words are such topics as wireless transmission of power, death rays, and radio-controlled airships. In addition, rare material on a secret city built at a remote jungle site in South America by one of Tesla's students, Guglielmo Marconi. Marconi's secret group claims to have built flying saucers in the 1940s and to have gone to Mars in the early 1950s! Incredible photos of these Tesla craft are included. •His plan to transmit free electricity into the atmosphere. •How electrical devices would work using only small antennas. •Why unlimited power could be utilized anywhere on earth. •How radio and radar technology can be used as death-ray weapons in Star Wars.
342 PAGES. 6x9 PAPERBACK. ILLUSTRATED. $16.95. CODE: FINT

REICH OF THE BLACK SUN
Nazi Secret Weapons & the Cold War Allied Legend
by Joseph P. Farrell

Why were the Allies worried about an atom bomb attack by the Germans in 1944? Why did the Soviets threaten to use poison gas against the Germans? Why did Hitler in 1945 insist that holding Prague could win the war for the Third Reich? Why did US General George Patton's Third Army race for the Skoda works at Pilsen in Czechoslovakia instead of Berlin? Why did the US Army not test the uranium atom bomb it dropped on Hiroshima? Why did the Luftwaffe fly a non-stop round trip mission to within twenty miles of New York City in 1944? *Reich of the Black Sun* takes the reader on a scientific-historical journey in order to answer these questions. Arguing that Nazi Germany actually won the race for the atom bomb in late 1944,

352 PAGES. 6x9 PAPERBACK. ILLUSTRATED. BIBLIOGRAPHY. $16.95. CODE: ROBS

THE GIZA DEATH STAR
The Paleophysics of the Great Pyramid & the Military Complex at Giza
by Joseph P. Farrell

Was the Giza complex part of a military installation over 10,000 years ago? Chapters include: An Archaeology of Mass Destruction, Thoth and Theories; The Machine Hypothesis; Pythagoras, Plato, Planck, and the Pyramid; The Weapon Hypothesis; Encoded Harmonics of the Planck Units in the Great Pyramid; High Freqguency Direct Current "Impulse" Technology; The Grand Gallery and its Crystals: Gravito-acoustic Resonators; The Other Two Large Pyramids; the "Causeways," and the "Temples"; A Phase Conjugate Howitzer; Evidence of the Use of Weapons of Mass Destruction in Ancient Times; more.

290 PAGES. 6x9 PAPERBACK. ILLUSTRATED. $16.95. CODE: GDS

THE GIZA DEATH STAR DEPLOYED
The Physics & Engineering of the Great Pyramid
by Joseph P. Farrell

Farrell expands on his thesis that the Great Pyramid was a maser, designed as a weapon and eventually deployed—with disastrous results to the solar system. Includes: Exploding Planets: A Brief History of the Exoteric and Esoteric Investigations of the Great Pyramid; No Machines, Please!; The Stargate Conspiracy; The Scalar Weapons; Message or Machine?; A Tesla Analysis of the Putative Physics and Engineering of the Giza Death Star; Cohering the Zero Point, Vacuum Energy, Flux: Feedback Loops and Tetrahedral Physics; and more.

290 PAGES. 6x9 PAPERBACK. ILLUSTRATED. $16.95. CODE: GDSD

THE GIZA DEATH STAR DESTROYED
The Ancient War For Future Science
by Joseph P. Farrell

Farrell moves on to events of the final days of the Giza Death Star and its awesome power. These final events, eventually leading up to the destruction of this giant machine, are dissected one by one, leading us to the eventual abandonment of the Giza Military Complex—an event that hurled civilization back into the Stone Age. Chapters include: The Mars-Earth Connection; The Lost "Root Races" and the Moral Reasons for the Flood; The Destruction of Krypton: The Electrodynamic Solar System, Exploding Planets and Ancient Wars; Turning the Stream of the Flood: the Origin of Secret Societies and Esoteric Traditions; The Quest to Recover Ancient Mega-Technology; Non-Equilibrium Paleophysics; Monatomic Paleophysics; Frequencies, Vortices and Mass Particles; "Acoustic" Intensity of Fields; The Pyramid of Crystals; tons more.

292 pages. 6x9 paperback. Illustrated. $16.95. Code: GDES

THE TESLA PAPERS
Nikola Tesla on Free Energy &
Wireless Transmission of Power
by Nikola Tesla, edited by David Hatcher Childress

David Hatcher Childress takes us into the incredible world of Nikola Tesla and his amazing inventions. Tesla's fantastic vision of the future, including wireless power, anti-gravity, free energy and highly advanced solar power. Also included are some of the papers, patents and material collected on Tesla at the Colorado Springs Tesla Symposiums, including papers on: •The Secret History of Wireless Transmission •Tesla and the Magnifying Transmitter •Design and Construction of a Half-Wave Tesla Coil •Electrostatics: A Key to Free Energy •Progress in Zero-Point Energy Research •Electromagnetic Energy from Antennas to Atoms •Tesla's Particle Beam Technology •Fundamental Excitatory Modes of the Earth-Ionosphere Cavity

325 PAGES. 8x10 PAPERBACK. ILLUSTRATED. $16.95. CODE: TTP

GRAVITATIONAL MANIPULATION OF DOMED CRAFT
UFO Propulsion Dynamics
by Paul E. Potter

Potter's precise and lavish illustrations allow the reader to enter directly into the realm of the advanced technological engineer and to understand, quite straightforwardly, the aliens' methods of energy manipulation: their methods of electrical power generation; how they purposely designed their craft to employ the kinds of energy dynamics that are exclusive to space (discoverable in our astrophysics) in order that their craft may generate both attractive and repulsive gravitational forces; their control over the mass-density matrix surrounding their craft enabling them to alter their physical dimensions and even manufacture their own frame of reference in respect to time. Includes a 16-page color insert.

624 pages. 7x10 Paperback. Illustrated. References. $24.00. Code: GMDC

TAPPING THE ZERO POINT ENERGY
Free Energy & Anti-Gravity in Today's Physics
by Moray B. King

King explains how free energy and anti-gravity are possible. The theories of the zero point energy maintain there are tremendous fluctuations of electrical field energy imbedded within the fabric of space. This book tells how, in the 1930s, inventor T. Henry Moray could produce a fifty kilowatt "free energy" machine; how an electrified plasma vortex creates anti-gravity; how the Pons/Fleischmann "cold fusion" experiment could produce tremendous heat without fusion; and how certain experiments might produce a gravitational anomaly.

180 PAGES. 5x8 PAPERBACK. ILLUSTRATED. $12.95. CODE: TAP

QUEST FOR ZERO-POINT ENERGY
Engineering Principles for "Free Energy"
by Moray B. King

King expands, with diagrams, on how free energy and anti-gravity are possible. The theories of zero point energy maintain there are tremendous fluctuations of electrical field energy embedded within the fabric of space. King explains the following topics: TFundamentals of a Zero-Point Energy Technology; Vacuum Energy Vortices; The Super Tube; Charge Clusters: The Basis of Zero-Point Energy Inventions; Vortex Filaments, Torsion Fields and the Zero-Point Energy; Transforming the Planet with a Zero-Point Energy Experiment; Dual Vortex Forms: The Key to a Large Zero-Point Energy Coherence. Packed with diagrams, patents and photos.

224 PAGES. 6x9 PAPERBACK. ILLUSTRATED. $14.95. CODE: QZPE

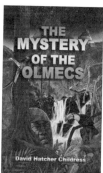

THE MYSTERY OF THE OLMECS
by David Hatcher Childress
The Olmecs were not acknowledged to have existed as a civilization until an international archeological meeting in Mexico City in 1942. Now, the Olmecs are slowly being recognized as the Mother Culture of Mesoamerica, having invented writing, the ball game and the "Mayan" Calendar. But who were the Olmecs? Where did they come from? What happened to them? How sophisticated was their culture? Why are many Olmec statues and figurines seemingly of foreign peoples such as Africans, Europeans and Chinese? Is there a link with Atlantis? In this heavily illustrated book, join Childress in search of the lost cities of the Olmecs! Chapters include: The Mystery of Quizuo; The Mystery of Transoceanic Trade; The Mystery of Cranial Deformation; more.
296 PAGES. 6x9 PAPERBACK. ILLUSTRATED. BIBLIOGRAPHY. COLOR SECTION. $20.00. CODE: MOLM

EYE OF THE PHOENIX
Mysterious Visions and
Secrets of the American Southwest
by Gary David
GaryDavid explores enigmas and anomalies in the vast American Southwest. Contents includes: The Great Pyramids of Arizona; Meteor Crater—Arizona's First Bonanza?; Chaco Canyon—Ancient City of the Dog Star; Phoenix—Masonic Metropolis in the Valley of the Sun; The Flying Shields of the Hopi Katsinam; Is the Starchild a Hopi God?; The Ant People of Orion—Ancient Star Beings of the Hopi; The Nagas—Origin of the Hopi Snake Clan?; The Tau (or T-shaped) Cross—Hopi/Maya/Egyptian Connections; The Hopi Stone Tablets of Techqua Ikachi; The Four Arms of Destiny and more.
348 pages. 6x9 Paperback. Illustrated. Bibliography. $16.95. Code: EOPX

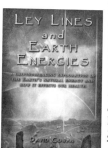

LEY LINE & EARTH ENERGIES
An Extraordinary Journey into the Earth's Natural Energy System
by David Cowan & Chris Arnold
The mysterious standing stones, burial grounds and stone circles that lace Europe, the British Isles and other areas have intrigued scientists, writers, artists and travellers through the centuries. How do ley lines work? How did our ancestors use Earth energy to map their sacred sites and burial grounds? How do ghosts and poltergeists interact with Earth energy? How can Earth spirals and black spots affect our health? This exploration shows how natural forces affect our behavior, how they can be used to enhance our health.
368 PAGES. 6x9 PAPERBACK. ILLUSTRATED. $18.95. CODE: LLEE

OTTO RAHN AND THE QUEST FOR THE HOLY GRAIL
The Amazing Life of the Real "Indiana Jones"
by Nigel Graddon
Otto Rahn led a life of incredible adventure in southern France in the early 1930s. The Hessian language scholar is said to have found runic Grail tablets in the Pyrenean grottoes, and decoded hidden messages within the medieval Grail masterwork *Parsifal*. The artifacts identified by Rahn were believed by Himmler to include the Grail Cup, the Spear of Destiny, the Tablets of Moses, the Ark of the Covenant, the Sword and Harp of David, the Sacred Candelabra and the Golden Urn of Manna. Some believe that Rahn was a Nazi guru who wielded immense influence on his elders and "betters" within the Hitler regime, persuading them that the Grail was the Sacred Book of the Aryans, which, once obtained, would justify their extreme political theories. But things are never as they seem, and as new facts emerge about Rahn a far more extraordinary story unfolds.
450 pages. 6x9 Paperback. Illustrated. Appendix. Index. $18.95. Code: ORQG

THE CRYSTAL SKULLS
Astonishing Portals to Man's Past
by David Hatcher Childress and Stephen S. Mehler

Childress introduces the technology and lore of crystals, and then plunges into the turbulent times of the Mexican Revolution form the backdrop for the rollicking adventures of Ambrose Bierce, the renowned journalist who went missing in the jungles in 1913, and F.A. Mitchell-Hedges, the notorious adventurer who emerged from the jungles with the most famous of the crystal skulls. Mehler shares his extensive knowledge of and experience with crystal skulls. Having been involved in the field since the 1980s, he has personally examined many of the most influential skulls, and has worked with the leaders in crystal skull research, including the inimitable Nick Nocerino, who developed a meticulous methodology for the purpose of examining the skulls.
294 pages. 6x9 Paperback. Illustrated. Bibliography. $18.95. Code: CRSK

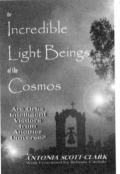

THE INCREDIBLE LIGHT BEINGS OF THE COSMOS
Are Orbs Intelligent Light Beings from the Cosmos?
by Antonia Scott-Clark

Scott-Clark has experienced orbs for many years, but started photographing them in earnest in the year 2000 when the "Light Beings" entered her life. She took these very seriously and set about privately researching orb occurrences. The incredible results of her findings are presented here, along with many of her spectacular photographs. With her friend, GoGos lead singer Belinda Carlisle, Antonia tells of her many adventures with orbs. Find the answers to questions such as: Can you see orbs with the naked eye?; Are orbs intelligent?; Antonia gives detailed instruction on how to photograph orbs, and how to communicate with these Light Beings of the Cosmos.
334 pages. 6x9 Paperback. Illustrated. References. $19.95. Code: ILBC

AXIS OF THE WORLD
The Search for the Oldest American Civilization
by Igor Witkowski

Polish author Witkowski's research reveals remnants of a high civilization that was able to exert its influence on almost the entire planet, and did so with full consciousness. Sites around South America show that this was not just one of the places influenced by this culture, but a place where they built their crowning achievements. Easter Island, in the southeastern Pacific, constitutes one of them. The Rongo-Rongo language that developed there points westward to the Indus Valley. Taken together, the facts presented by Witkowski provide a fresh, new proof that an antediluvian, great civilization flourished several millennia ago.
220 pages. 6x9 Paperback. Illustrated. References. $18.95. Code: AXOW

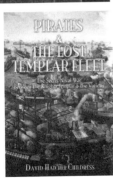

PIRATES & THE LOST TEMPLAR FLEET
by David Hatcher Childress

Childress takes us into the fascinating world of maverick sea captains who were Knights Templar (and later Scottish Rite Free Masons) who battled the ships that sailed for the Pope. The lost Templar fleet was originally based at La Rochelle in southern France, but fled to the deep fiords of Scotland upon the dissolution of the Order by King Phillip. This banned fleet of ships was later commanded by the St. Clair family of Rosslyn Chapel (birthplace of Free Masonry). St. Clair and his Templars made a voyage to Canada in the year 1298 AD, nearly 100 years before Columbus! Later, this fleet of ships and new ones to come, flew the Skull and Crossbones, the symbol of the Knights Templar.
320 PAGES. 6x9 PAPERBACK. ILLUSTRATED. BIBLIOGRAPHY. $16.95. CODE: PLTF

ORDER FORM

**10% Discount
When You Order
3 or More Items!**

One Adventure Place
P.O. Box 74
Kempton, Illinois 60946
United States of America
Tel.: 815-253-6390 • Fax: 815-253-6300
Email: auphq@frontiernet.net
http://www.adventuresunlimitedpress.com

ORDERING INSTRUCTIONS

✓ Remit by USD$ Check, Money Order or Credit Card

✓ Visa, Master Card, Discover & AmEx Accepted

✓ Paypal Payments Can Be Made To:

　info@wexclub.com

✓ Prices May Change Without Notice

✓ 10% Discount for 3 or more Items

SHIPPING CHARGES

United States

✓ Postal Book Rate { $4.00 First Item / 50¢ Each Additional Item

✓ POSTAL BOOK RATE Cannot Be Tracked!

✓ Priority Mail { $5.00 First Item / $2.00 Each Additional Item

✓ UPS { $6.00 First Item / $1.50 Each Additional Item

　NOTE: UPS Delivery Available to Mainland USA Only

Canada

✓ Postal Air Mail { $10.00 First Item / $2.50 Each Additional Item

✓ Personal Checks or Bank Drafts MUST BE

　US$ and Drawn on a US Bank

✓ Canadian Postal Money Orders OK

✓ Payment MUST BE US$

All Other Countries

✓ Sorry, No Surface Delivery!

✓ Postal Air Mail { $16.00 First Item / $6.00 Each Additional Item

✓ Checks and Money Orders MUST BE US$
　and Drawn on a US Bank or branch.

✓ Paypal Payments Can Be Made in US$ To:
　info@wexclub.com

SPECIAL NOTES

✓ RETAILERS: Standard Discounts Available

✓ BACKORDERS: We Backorder all Out-of-
　Stock Items Unless Otherwise Requested

✓ PRO FORMA INVOICES: Available on Request

ORDER ONLINE AT: www.adventuresunlimitedpress.com

Please check: ✓

☐ This is my first order　　☐ I have ordered before

Name

Address

City

State/Province　　　　　　Postal Code

Country

Phone day　　　　　　　Evening

Fax　　　　　Email

Item Code	Item Description	Qty	Total

Please check: ✓

Subtotal ▶

Less Discount-10% for 3 or more items ▶

☐ Postal-Surface　　　　　　Balance ▶

☐ Postal-Air Mail　Illinois Residents 6.25% Sales Tax ▶

　(Priority in USA)　　　　Previous Credit ▶

☐ UPS　　　　　　　　　Shipping ▶

　(Mainland USA only) Total (check/MO in USD$ only) ▶

☐ Visa/MasterCard/Discover/American Express

Card Number

Expiration Date

10% Discount When You Order 3 or More Items!